STUDENT GRUB

Alastair Williams

summersdale

STUDENT GRUB

1st edition printed in 1991, reprinted 1992 and 1993
2nd edition printed in 1995
3rd edition printed in 2000, 2001 and 2003
This 4th edition copyright © Alastair Williams 2004

Summersdale Publishers Ltd
46 West Street
Chichester
West Sussex
PO19 1RP
United Kingdom

www.summersdale.com

ISBN 1 84024 405 4

Printed at Cox and Wyman, Reading, England

To my parents
with love and thanks

Alastair Williams was a student at numerous establishments of higher education before eventually graduating from Southampton. He has travelled throughout the world in his quest for mouth-watering recipes that can easily be reproduced by any student, and this book is the result.

CONTENTS

INTRODUCTION

WHAT'S ALL THIS COOKING STUFF ABOUT?

Starting University

Higher education is supposed to do more than improve a person academically: time spent at college will give students an opportunity to experience a wide range of activities and to mature as an adult . . . well, that's the theory anyway.

Starting college in new surroundings with new people can be daunting; for those leaving the comfort and security of their home for the first time it may take some getting used to.

On the other hand there are those who can't wait to leave home, to escape from parents who always complain about loud music or untidy bedrooms. Arrival at college means that you have the freedom to do what you want, within certain physical and legal parameters.

Unfortunately, leaving home has its disadvantages. For example, you'll soon miss certain things: home cooking, someone to do the washing, someone to tidy up after you, and a parent's car with a full tank of petrol. Whether you are sharing a house, living in a self-catering flat, or even in halls of residence, you'll have to learn to cope for yourself. This means cooking.

Food may well be a problem, and mistakes will be made in trying to solve it. Many students initially opt to live on takeaways, but there is a limit to how many chicken vindaloos your stomach can take, and precious grants can soon dwindle.

STUDENT GRUB

Aims of the Book

It may seem that all is lost, but there is an alternative – pick up this book and get cooking. The object of this book is to give students a selection of recipes and advice that will enable them to get beyond the realms of cheese on toast or shrivelled jacket potatoes and to discover simple but tasty dishes. (Those who have yet to reach the realms of cheese on toast will nevertheless find ample recipes to get them going.)

The majority of the recipes in this book are designed to be cheap and easy to prepare, but there is also a section on more adventurous meals and advice on entertaining. This book is in no way trying to compete with the higher end of the culinary spectrum. There are numerous fine cookbooks available that will tell you how to cook dishes such as pigeon breast stuffed with ceps, or how to prepare lagoustine drizzled with truffle oil. This book is aimed at students and the budgetary constraints which they will no doubt be under. Fine ingredients are expensive, and even items such as a small bunch of basil might be considered a luxury by many. It would be nice to recommend that you only buy organic this and that, but the reality is that you will want to keep your food spend to a minimum.

The emphasis of the book is on preparing and cooking main courses, but starters are included for those wanting to impress. And, of course, the all-important sections on desserts and cakes, plus snacks and breakfasts cover most eventualities.

INTRODUCTION

What You Need

The chances are that your kitchen, as well as being a health liability, will lack the modern appliances that most family kitchens have. The idea of attempting a meal without a Magimix and its 101 attachments may seem daunting, but it can be done. From personal experience I know that most student kitchens will not even have a set of scales, so many of the measurements given use spoons, and where ounces and grams are used the amounts can often be converted using the chart that turns imperial and metric into more usable table- and teaspoons.

You may also need patience. Many of the recipes given are quick and simple, but when attempting something more adventurous it is essential not to give up. There are going to be times when your soufflé looks more like a pancake, but even the best chefs have the occasional disaster.

Some people will find cooking very easy, but they're probably swots anyway. The rest of us mere mortals need a little more perseverance and patience. But cooking disasters are all part of the fun, and experimenting with this book could lead to all sorts of wonderful experiences, some of which may even be of a culinary nature.

THE BASICS

If you have had no experience of cooking (and judging from some of my friends who lived for three years on baked beans and toast, without the wit even to combine the two, this is entirely possible) then you will need some help. Unfortunately, most cookery books tend to be marketed towards those who have experience in cooking, and they contain far too many irrelevant, expensive, impractical and unpalatable recipes for students. What would your housemates think if you were to serve them a platter of marinated pigs' trotters? Rest assured, there are no monkey brains or goats' testicles to be found in this book. Much like in a restaurant, it is the quality of food, the friendliness of the service and the general ambience that can provide a perfect meal – not frilly tablecloths, crystal glasses and extortionate prices.

Common Sense

The recipes in this book are designed with simplicity in mind, both in terms of implements and cooking skills required. All that is needed is common sense – I don't want to be held responsible for a student who ends up in the hospital burns department for having misunderstood the instruction 'stand in boiling water for 20 minutes'.

Another important point to remember is that all cooking times and heats are approximate. Cooking is an instinctive thing and no number of instructions can replace common sense and initiative.

There are a wide variety of recipes in this book. They range from cheap to expensive, from easy to prepare to being moderately difficult. The emphasis is on simple but interesting meals.

THE BASICS

Before you try any recipe, read through it first to make sure you have all the ingredients and equipment as well as the time to prepare it.

Here are some basic reminders, hints and guidelines for the beginner. Refer back to these basics when cooking full recipes.

How to Cook Rice

There are various types of rice available, but if you are trying to save your grant then buy the cheapest. Allow about 2 to 3 oz (50 to 75g) per person. If you don't have any scales, a mug holds about 8 oz (200g), so use that as a guideline.

Before cooking rice it is advisable to put it in a sieve and wash it. This removes some of the starch and will help to prevent it from sticking. After washing the rice, place it in a saucepan with a covering of water and cook according to the instructions on the packet. The time it takes depends on the type of rice used. The best way of testing it is to taste it. If it is still hard in the middle it needs a bit longer. Make sure that there is enough water in the saucepan, otherwise it will burn on the bottom.

Pasta

Allow roughly 2 oz (50g) of pasta per person. See the Italian section on cooking pasta.

How to Cook Potatoes

Chips, crisps, mash – need I say more about the versatility of this deceptively plain-looking discovery of Sir Walter? Here are some guidelines for cooking the perfect tater.

STUDENT GRUB

There are two basic types of potato: new and old. Both are available all year round. Allow 1 or 2 potatoes per person, depending on your appetite and the size of the potato.

All potatoes need to peeled or scrubbed before cooking, unless you are preparing jacket potatoes.

There are many different ways in which you can cook potatoes. The most common way is to boil them. After peeling or scrubbing the potatoes, cut into halves or quarters, depending on their size, then place in salted boiling water for 15 to 20 minutes or until they are tender all the way through. If you want mashed potato make sure they are well cooked otherwise they will be lumpy. Drain the potatoes, add a nob of butter and a drop of milk, then using a potato masher squash until they are nice and creamy, adding more milk and some black pepper if required.

If you want to prepare a more exotic mash, you can add a teaspoon of smooth french mustard and some finely chopped fresh rosemary.

Roast Potatoes

Peel the potatoes, then halve or quarter them depending on their size. Parboil (this means they are only partially boiled) for 5 minutes in salted boiling water, then drain. Place the semi-cooked potatoes in a baking tray with some oil and stick in the oven on Gas Mark 6 (425 °F, 220 °C) near the top of the oven if possible. Baste the potatoes with the oil a couple times while they are cooking. Roast the potatoes until they are golden and verging on crispiness, this should take between 60 and 90 minutes.

THE BASICS

Chips

These things are almost a British institution, and they should of course be served with fish and wrapped in an old newspaper with lashings of vinegar and salt. If that description hasn't quelled your craving for chips then here is how to make your own.

Peel some old potatoes and cut into chip shapes. If you are feeling sophisticated slice them more thinly into French fries. The next stage is potentially dangerous so take care. The chips need to be covered or at least partially covered in oil to cook, so a large amount of oil is needed.

Heat the oil in a large frying pan, then carefully add the chips, taking care not to throw them in the pan, otherwise hot oil will be splashed.

Fry the chips until they are crisp, making sure that the oil does not get too hot.

Whatever you do remember to turn the heat off. If your fat does catch fire it is imperative that you do the right thing.

The Right Thing

• Never throw water on top of the oil – this will make it worse.

• Turn off the gas if you can safely do so, otherwise wait until the fire has been extinguished.

• The most effective way to put out a fat fire is to get a dampened tea towel and place it over the top of the pan. Leave it there until all the flames are gone.

Hygiene

If you are in a large shared house, the kitchen may have to cope with as many as seven, eight or nine people. Sometimes the kitchen also serves as the communal room. It is quite easy when there are large numbers of people sharing a small kitchen for it to become quite disgusting. Having been a student for a number of years I have had the opportunity to visit many student kitchens, and most of them were truly revolting – the washing up was normally only done when there were no more spare plates or cutlery available, or when parents or landlords came to visit.

It is a good idea if you are in a shared house to organise some sort of rota for cooking and cleaning. If one or two people cook each night for everyone it avoids the hassle that would occur if everybody in the house waited to use the cooker for themselves. It also means that you will only be cooking perhaps once or twice a week.

When your kitchen gets to the stage where you are sharing it with the rats and cockroaches, it's time to start worrying. Food that is left lying around for long enough will go off and harmful bacteria will evolve. If the green furry parts in your kitchen make it look more like a biology experiment than a hygienic place suitable for food storage and preparation, it might be a good idea to clear the whole kitchen and disinfect it.

Apart from having clean kitchen surfaces, it is essential that the fridge is looked after too. If something is spilt make sure it is mopped up, and not left to fester.

It is important when buying meat that it is eaten within the recommended time on the packaging. If there is no label ask the supermarket assistant or butcher. The above applies not only to meat but to all products that have a limited life, such as eggs, yoghurt etc.

CONVERSION CHART

The recipes in this book are given in imperial and metric measurements, which are self explanatory, but many small amounts are measured in terms of spoons or cups.

The following abbreviations are used:

tbs = **tablespoon** (the one that's too big to put in your mouth)
tsp = **teaspoon** (what you put in your teacup)

Spoon measures can also be substituted for ounces with certain ingredients, which is handy for those without a set of kitchen scales. Obviously the weights of all ingredients will vary, but here are some rough measures:

1 tbs   = 1 oz (25g) of . . . syrup, jam, honey etc
2 tbs   = 1 oz (25g) of . . . butter, margarine, sugar
3 tbs   = 1 oz (25g) of . . . cornflour, cocoa, custard, flour
4 tbs   = 1 oz (25g) of . . . grated cheese, porridge oats

All spoon measures refer to **level** spoons, not heaped.
1 mug of rice weighs roughly 8 oz (200g)

The approximations used for conversion between metric and imperial in this book are as follows:

1 oz	=	25g
1 lb	=	500g
1 fluid oz	=	25ml
1 pint	=	0.5 litre
1 inch	=	2.5 cm

In all recipes the oven should be heated to the temperature stated prior to cooking.

GLOSSARY OF COOKING TERMS

Baste   To spoon fat or oil over food to keep it moist. Usually done to a joint of meat whilst it is in the oven.

Beat   This is the mixing of ingredients using a wooden spoon, a fork or a whisk.

Chop   To cut into small pieces.

Cream   To mix fat with another ingredient like sugar until it becomes creamy.

Dice   To cut into small cubes.

Grate   A grater can produce coarse or fine shavings of food, such as cheese or vegetables.

Knead   To use your knuckles to smooth dough out, the idea being to get a smooth texture.

Marinade   A combination of juices, spices and oils in which meat is soaked to enhance the flavour.

Parboil   This is the partial boiling of something. The cooking of the food will then normally be finished off by another method, i.e. roast potatoes.

Peel   To remove the skin or the outer layer of a vegetable.

Rub in   To rub flour and fat together between your fingertips until they resemble breadcrumbs.

Simmer   To cook just below the boiling point, so that only an occasional bubble appears on the surface.

HEALTHY EATING

Healthy eating is something that many of us pay little thought to – youthful decadence is more fun, after all. But if your idea of a balanced diet means equal amounts of food to alcohol you should read this section.

Normally, when living at home and eating three square meals a day (presumably including plenty of vegetables and fruit), you will receive all the vitamins and minerals needed to stay healthy. All this can change when you go away to college. It is very easy to start skipping meals – most people I knew who lived in halls very rarely had breakfast, took only a sandwich or some chocolate for a quick, filling lunch, and then perhaps a baked potato with chips for dinner. This is not particularly healthy.

Those living in a shared house will find cooking easier than those living on their own: you can take turns to cook, and it is much easier and more enjoyable cooking for a group than for just one. If you are living on your own try and find someone else to share meals with. Cooking for one is less efficient and less economical, and it can be hard to put in much effort.

Eating food does much more than fill your belly. It provides the energy for movement, allows the healing of wounds and instigates the production of protoplasm which helps to replace dead cells.

If you want to stay healthy you must have a balanced diet. There are certain things that are essential to obtaining this.

STUDENT GRUB

Carbohydrates

These are the provider of energy. They also happen to be the cheapest types of food and can be found in things like potatoes, bread and rice. Although these foods are always available in ample supply, take care to limit your own intake because an excess of carbohydrates leads to obesity.

Fats

These also provide energy for the body, but they take longer to digest than carbohydrates. This means they are useful for storing energy. Fat is present in dairy products like butter, margarine, milk, cheese and, of course, in meat.

Proteins

The word protein derives from the Greek word 'of first importance', and that is exactly what they are. Proteins are necessary for bodily development and repairs to damaged cells. Proteins are found in fish, lean meat, milk, cheese and eggs.

Vitamins

This is one area where many students fail to supply the correct amounts vital to keeping the body in perfect running order. The following is a list of the most essential vitamins and their sources:

Vitamin A

Vitamin A is present in dairy products like cheese, butter and milk, and in green vegetables and liver.

Vitamin B

Vitamin B is made up of more than 10 different vitamins. They are to be found in whole grain cereals, liver, yeast and lean meat.

Vitamin C

In the days of Nelson, scurvy was a common problem for a ship's crew. This is a disease resulting from a lack of vitamin C. The main source of the vitamin is citrus fruits like lemons and oranges, and blackcurrants and fresh vegetables. Vitamin C is great for the immune system and helps to protect against the common cold.

Vitamin D

A deficiency in calcium can lead to rickets in children, which means the bones are weak. In adults it can result in bow-legs. Vitamin D is found in milk, butter, cheese and liver.

Vitamin E

This is a vitamin that does not usually pose a deficiency problem in our society. It is found in milk, cheese, butter and meat.

Vitamin K

This is found in green vegetables. It helps the blood clotting process.

Roughage

This is vital if you want to keep all your passages open, or if you are having trouble making substantial deposits. High fibre cereals provide a good source of roughage.

STUDENT GRUB

Water

It may seem obvious that the body requires a substantial amount of water to function, but in case you forget this is a reminder.

Minerals

There are three main minerals whose continued supply can all too easily be jeopardised: iron, calcium and iodine. Other minerals such as the phosphates, potassium, magnesium and sodium are generally in good supply.

Iron

This is vital for the formation of the red blood cells. If a person has a deficiency of iron it can lead to anaemia. This is a shortage of red blood cells. Ensuring a high iron intake is not as simple as eating a bag of nails, however. Far better to eat liver, which is slightly more palatable, and is an excellent source of iron, as are other meats.

Calcium

This mineral is important for strong bones and teeth. It is found in dairy products like milk, butter and cheese.

Iodine

Iodine, although important, is not needed in the same quantities as calcium or iron. Fish is a good source of iodine.

Minerals and vitamins are available in pills from healthfood shops and supermarkets. Some contain multi vitamins, while others are more specific. It is still important to follow the recommended dosage.

THE STORE CUPBOARD

It is a common problem when cooking that whatever ingredients you have in your cupboard will always be the things you don't need, while whatever you do need will be conspicuous by its absence. You will also find that certain things in your cupboard will disappear almost immediately, like choccy biscuits, whilst Grandma's home-made chutney will stay lurking in the depths of the cupboard until you change house, or until the contents of the jar are used as a loose floortile adhesive.

Here is a suggested list of useful things to have in your cupboard:

Cans

Apart from the obligatory cans of lager, canned food is always useful for its longevity, and whole meals can often be prepared from one can.

Examples:
- Tomatoes *(used constantly throughout this book)*
- Sweetcorn
- Tuna
- Coconut milk
- Spaghetti (in tomato juice)
- Baked beans
- Ravioli
- Chick peas
- Kidney beans
- Soups
- Lentils

STUDENT GRUB

Dry Goods

Cereals:	• Weetabix
	• Cornflakes
	• Bran flakes
	• Porridge oats
Flour:	• Self-raising
	• Plain
Pasta:	• Spaghetti
	• Tagliatelli
	• Shells
	• Tortellini
	• Quills
	• Penne
Dried Fruits:	• Sultanas
	• Currants
	• Raisins
	• Glacé cherries
Nuts:	• Almonds
	• Walnuts
Rice:	• Long grain
	• Basmati
Sugars:	• Caster
	• Granulated or golden granulated
	• Brown
	• Icing
Coconut:	• Desiccated
	• Soluble
Packet sauces:	• Bread
	• Cheese
	• Parsley

VEGETABLES

It's all too easy to leave out vegetables from a low budget diet: students often fail to balance their diet in this respect. The only vegetable with which they are familiar is usually the 'couch potato'.

Prepared to mend your ways? Rather than sticking with humdrum peas and carrots, try experimenting with the more exotic vegetables that are available in supermarkets these days.

Below is a list of some of the common and not-so-common vegetables currently available, explaining how they should be prepared and various ways of cooking them.

Aubergine This is a purplish marrow. Cut the top and bottom off and then slice thinly. Sprinkle lightly with salt and leave for 10 minutes. Before cooking, rinse the slices in water. The usual method for cooking aubergines is to fry them either in oil or butter until they soften.

Baby Sweetcorn These are an expensive import from the Orient, but as with mangetout they are worth the price. The only preparation needed is washing, following which they can be gently boiled or fried. To benefit from their full flavour they need to retain their crispness.

Beans (French) Wash them and top and tail. Cut into 1-inch lengths, or leave whole. To cook place in boiling water with a little salt and cook for 10 to 15 minutes. After cooking they can be tossed in butter.

STUDENT GRUB

Broccoli Wash in cold water, cut off the stalks then divide into flowerets. That means breaking off into clumps. Cook in salted boiling water for about 7 minutes. It is important not to over-cook broccoli because it will go mushy and lose most of its flavour.

Brussels Sprouts Remove the outer leaves and cut off the stalk. It should not be removed entirely, otherwise all the leaves will fall off. Cut a cross into the base and then wash in cold water. Cook in salted boiling water for about 10 minutes.

Cabbage There are three main varieties of cabbage: green, white and red. Remove the tough outer leaves and the centre stalk. You can either shred the leaves or perhaps quarter them. To cook the shredded cabbage place in boiling water for about 5 minutes. If the leaves are bigger they will need about 10 minutes.

Carrots Top and tail the carrots and then either using a peeler or a knife remove the outer surface. Before cooking they can be quartered or sliced. Baby carrots can be cooked whole. Cook in boiling water for about 15 minutes. Carrots can be eaten raw in salads etc. They can also be roasted in oil when cooking a roast dinner.

Cauliflower Wash in cold water and then divide into flowerets. Cook in salted boiling water until tender – this should take about 10 minutes, depending on the size of the flowerets. Cauliflower can also be eaten raw and used for crudités at parties.

VEGETABLES

Courgettes Having been force-fed these things for years I have almost come to like them. First of all give them a wash, then top and tail them. Slice thinly and fry in butter or oil for about 10 minutes.

Leeks Definitely a favourite with the Welsh. Remove the top dark green bit and the roots and wash. They can either be sliced into rings, quartered or even left whole. To cook either boil for 10 to 15 minutes or fry in oil or butter for about 10 minutes.

Mangetout If you haven't seen these before, they look like pea pods that have been squashed by a lorry. But they taste delicious and are almost worth the extortionate amount you will be charged for them.

To prepare your mangetout, wash and top and tail them. If boiling them, they need only 3 or 4 minutes because they maintain their flavour better when still crisp. They can also be fried gently in butter for a few minutes until they soften slightly. They make a colourful addition to stir fries.

Mushrooms If you are studying near the countryside you could try and find some wild mushrooms, but I don't mean those of the Paul Daniels variety (no recipes for space cakes in this book). Be careful not to pick any toadstools.

Anyway, once you have found or bought your mushrooms, wipe them with a clean damp cloth. Either remove or trim the stalk and then slice or leave whole. The mushrooms can be fried or grilled. To fry, heat a little oil or butter in a frying pan and cook for about 3 to 4 minutes, depending on size. To grill, put under a hot grill with a light covering of butter.

Onions The best way to stop your eyes watering when chopping onions is to get someone else to do it. Top and tail the onion first, then peel off the outer layer. It can be chopped or sliced into rings. Onions are normally fried in oil for about 5 minutes.

Parsnips Top and tail, then peel and chop into largish pieces or thick slices. They can be boiled, fried or roasted.

To boil, place in boiling water with a pinch of salt for about 20 minutes or until they are tender.

If they are to be fried they need to be cut into thin slices or chips, otherwise they will not cook all the way through.

Perhaps the nicest way of cooking parsnips is to bake them. Place the parsnips in an ovenproof dish with a couple of tablespoons of oil and bake in a hot oven for about 40 minutes. They can be basted as if they were roast potatoes.

Peas If you have fresh peas, ie still in the pod, shell them and wash in cold water. To cook peas, place them in boiling water for about 10 minutes.

Peppers The most commonly available peppers are the red and green ones, although there are yellow and orange varieties. They all have different flavours – the lighter in colour they are the sweeter they are, so the yellow ones are the sweetest and the green ones the most bitter.

Top and tail, then core and remove all the seeds. Slice into rings then halve and fry in a little oil for 5 minutes or so. They can also be eaten raw and are particularly nice in salads.

Potatoes See **Basics.**

Pumpkin If you have a whole pumpkin, cut into 4 then remove all the seeds and pulp from the inside. Remove the skin and cut into chunks. To boil, place in salted boiling water for about 30 minutes.

After the pumpkin has been boiled it can be fried in butter for 5 minutes.

Spinach The magic green weed that did wonders for Popeye hasn't yet had much effect on me! When buying spinach, buy more than you would if it was cabbage, as spinach will shrink considerably during cooking. Discard any yellowed leaves, then place in a small amount of boiling water for about 5 minutes. Grated nutmeg and spinach taste good together.

Swede Although this is not perhaps a vegetable you would normally choose to cook, it can provide an interesting alternative to 'chips and that'. Peel and chop into chunks, then wash in cold water. Cook in salted boiling water for 20 to 25 minutes or until tender. Can be mashed with a nob of butter and black pepper.

Sweetcorn Remove the husks and the ends, then place in boiling water for 10 minutes. Drain, then serve with butter and fresh black pepper.

Tomato Fresh tomatoes can be fried in butter or grilled. To remove the skin of a tomato, which should be done when making sauces, place in boiling water for about a minute. Remove from the hot water and cool them in cold water. The skins should now come away easily.

SPICES, HERBS AND SEASONINGS

Given moderate use, these can transform a plain tasting meal into something special. Just remember the amounts used have to be carefully controlled, the idea being to enhance the flavour of the food, not to annihilate your taste buds.

When a recipe includes 'salt and pepper' it generally means a pinch of each, but it is up to the individual to season according to taste. One of the most essential items in a kitchen should be a pepper mill. Freshly ground pepper tastes so much better than the stuff that is pre-ground, so try and get hold of one. Here are the most commonly-used spices, herbs and seasonings:

Basil	Flavourings	Parsley
Bay leaves	Essences	Paprika pepper
Black pepper	Garlic	Rosemary
Capers	Garam masala	Sage
Caraway seeds	Ginger	Salt
Cayenne seeds	Lemon juice	Soy sauce
Chillies	Mace	Sweet and sour sauce
Chilli powder	Marjoram	Tabasco sauce
Chutney	Mint	Thyme
Chives	Mustard: French	Worcester sauce
Cinnamon	English	Vinegar: cider
Cloves	Oregano	malt
Curry powder	Nutmeg	wine

DRESSINGS AND SAUCES

The use of sauces and dressings can provide an exciting accompaniment to many otherwise plain tasting dishes.

CHEESE SAUCE

This sauce is used in many of the recipes in this book, such as lasagne or cauliflower cheese.

Ingredients

1 pint (0.5 litre) of milk
4 oz (100g) of grated cheese
2 oz (50g) of butter
2 oz (50g) of plain flour
Salt
Pepper

Melt the butter in a small saucepan, but don't let it brown. Then stir in the flour and cook gently for a couple of minutes. The combination of butter and flour is called a roux, and it is also the name of the method of preparation.

Remove the roux from the heat and add a little of the milk. It has to be added gradually otherwise it will end up being lumpy. Stir the milk in until a smooth consistency is achieved, then add the rest of the milk. When all the milk has been added return the pan to the heat, add the cheese and bring to the boil. Simmer for five minutes or so until the sauce has thickened.

PARSLEY SAUCE

This sauce is normally served with fish, but can be served with almost anything. The quantity can be halved if a smaller amount is needed.

Ingredients

1 pint (0.5 litre) of milk
2 oz (50g) of plain flour
2 oz (50g) of butter
4 tbs of chopped fresh parsley
Salt
Pepper

The method for this sauce is as for the previous recipe, except the parsley is added just before serving.

FRENCH DRESSING

There are many variations of French dressing, and most people have their own favourite combinations. Olive oil is a must for an authentic tasting dressing – vegetable oil, although much cheaper, will not taste as good. Here are a few ideas . . .

It is unlikely that you are going to need vast quantities of the stuff so as a guideline use 4 parts olive oil to 1 part wine vinegar. A dash of French mustard, pepper, oregano or lemon juice can be added for more flavour. Place all the ingredients together in a small screw-top jar, and shake to combine the flavours.

YOGHURT DRESSING

Ingredients

¼ pint (125ml) of plain yoghurt
1 tbs of lemon juice
Salt
Pepper

Mix the yoghurt and lemon juice together. Season according to taste.

PESTO

This recipe uses insane quantities of fresh basil, but the aroma is intoxicating. Pesto is traditionally served with pasta, but it can be spread on toast.

Serves 4

Ingredients

2 cloves of garlic, peeled and crushed
2 oz (50g) of pine nuts
2 cups of fresh basil leaves
3 tbs of finely grated fresh parmesan
¼ pint (125ml) of olive oil
Salt

Put the basil leaves, pine nuts and garlic in a blender and grind for a few seconds. Then add the cheese, oil and salt and mix well. If you are a stickler for authenticity, then you should prepare the pesto in a mortar, but a blender is far quicker.

SOUPS AND STARTERS

Also known, though not in student circles, as entrées and hors d'oeuvres. Guaranteed to shock your dinner guests into thinking that you have been somewhat frugal with the grub, it is important to emphasise that this is only a starter, so that they realise the extent of your sophistication.

These dishes are obviously intended for special occasions, and are not designed to fit in with the typical weekly budget. But the soup recipes can make a filling meal in themselves, and simply by increasing the portions some of the other recipes can be served as main dishes.

GARLIC BREAD

This has to be another classic student recipe, though its resultant effect on the breath can limit one's amorous aspirations.

Ingredients

**French stick
6 oz (150g) of butter
2 cloves of garlic**

Put the butter in a small mixing bowl. Finely chop the garlic and add to the butter, blending it in with a fork. Slice the French stick at 2-inch intervals, without actually severing it, and spread some of the butter on both sides of each slit. Then close up the gaps and wrap the loaf in foil. Place in the oven and cook for 15 to 20 minutes at Gas Mark 5 (400 °F, 200 °C).

MUSHROOMS WITH GARLIC BUTTER

Garlic again . . . well, you either love it or hate it.

Ingredients

**4 oz (100g) of mushrooms
4 oz (100g) of butter
2 cloves of garlic, peeled and finely chopped**

Remove the stalk of the mushrooms then wash. Dry the mushrooms with kitchen paper. Mix the butter and the garlic together with a fork and then spread on top of the mushrooms. Bake in the oven for 15 minutes at Gas Mark 5 (400 °F, 200 °C).

MINI SAUSAGES WITH HONEY AND ROSEMARY

This has to be one of my favourite dishes – just writing about it makes me drool! Fresh rosemary is a must, though.

Ingredients

**Pack of mini sausages
Handful of fresh rosemary
3 tbs of runny honey**

Arrange the sausages in a baking dish, prick with a fork, spoon on the honey, then place the rosemary on top. Bake in the oven at Gas Mark 6 (425 °F, 220 °C) for about 25 minutes, turning occasionally so they brown evenly.

HUMMUS

This one is a dip that can be served with freshly chopped vegetables (crudités) or pitta bread. Although hummus is available ready-made or even from your local delicatessen, it is cheaper to make your own. Having said that, I find it easier to use canned chick peas instead of soaking dried ones for hours. Note that a blender is needed for this recipe.

Ingredients

1 can of chick peas
2 cloves of garlic, peeled and finely chopped
Juice of 1 lemon
2 tbs of olive oil
4 oz (100g) of natural unsweetened yoghurt
½ tsp of ground cumin

Put all the ingredients in a blender and let them have it! Switch off when a soft consistency is achieved. Then put in a dish and chill for an hour or two.

CARROT AND GINGER SOUP

This is my favourite of all soups; the ginger gives it a delicious flavour that never fails to impress. Use fresh ginger, but remember to take it out before serving.

Serves 4

Ingredients

1 lb (500g) of carrots, peeled and chopped
1 potato, peeled and quartered
1 piece of fresh root ginger, peeled and chopped
2 pints (1 litre) water
2 tbs single cream (optional)
Salt
Pepper

Place the carrots, potato and ginger in a pan and cover with the water. Bring to the boil and then simmer for 20 minutes. Remove from the heat and take out the ginger. Transfer the ingredients into a blender and blend until a smooth consistency is achieved. Season according to taste and stir in the cream if desired.

TOMATO SOUP

Serves 4

Ingredients

I lb (500g) of tomatoes
I onion, peeled and finely chopped
I bay leaf
I oz (25g) of flour
I pint (0.5 litre) of water
½ pint (0.25 litre) of milk
I tbs of olive oil
Salt
Pepper

Boil some water in a saucepan, then place the tomatoes in it. Remove the pan from heat and leave for about 5 minutes. Take the tomatoes from the water and peel off the skins. Chop into small pieces.

Using a large saucepan, fry the tomatoes and onion gently in the oil for about 15 minutes until they go mushy. Add the water and the bay leaf, then simmer for 1 hour. If you don't want bits in your soup you can sieve it. Otherwise, just add the flour and milk to the tomato mixture. Simmer for about 3 minutes, then serve.

FRENCH ONION SOUP

The French are passionate about their soups, and most regions have their own speciality soup which reflects the area, climate and produce. With this recipe there are no firm rules and numerous variations on the same theme occur. This is one soup that benefits from using home-made beef stock.

Serves 4

Ingredients

**2 large onions, peeled and thinly sliced
2 pints (1 litre) of beef stock
2 tsp of flour
1 tbs of olive oil
4 slices of French bread
2 oz (50g) of Gruyère cheese, grated
Salt
Pepper**

Heat the oil in a saucepan, then fry the onions slowly for 15 minutes, until they are a golden colour. Stir in the flour and cook for about 5 minutes, stirring the onions constantly. Add the beef stock and bring to the boil. Season and simmer for 25 minutes. Preheat the grill. Divide the cheese onto the slices of bread. When the soup is ready pour it into a serving dish (to be authentic you should have an earthenware tureen), place the slices of bread on top of the soup and put under the grill until the cheese melts. Serve immediately.

VEGETABLE SOUP

There are no limits as to what vegetables you can use. These are just a guideline.

Serves 4

Ingredients

2 tbs of olive oil
I onion, peeled and chopped
I leek, thinly sliced
2 cabbage leaves, shredded or finely chopped
I courgette, finely chopped
I carrot, peeled and sliced
I bay leaf
2 pints (I litre) of vegetable stock
Salt
Pepper

Heat the oil in a large saucepan, then fry the onion for about 5 minutes or until it has softened. Then add the other vegetables and fry for a further 10 minutes. Add the stock, season, bring to the boil, then simmer for 30 minutes. Remove the bay leaf before serving. If you want a smoother tasting soup then liquidise before serving.

PARSNIP AND APPLE SOUP

A liquidiser is required for this recipe.

Serves 4

Ingredients

2 tbs of oil
I large onion, peeled and chopped
I ½ lb (750g) parsnips, peeled and chopped
I apple, peeled and cored
2 pints (I litre) of vegetable stock
Salt
Pepper

Heat the oil in a large saucepan, then fry the onion for about 5 minutes until it has softened. Add the apple and the parsnips and fry gently for a couple of minutes. Add the stock and bring to the boil, then simmer for 30 minutes. Transfer the soup into a liquidiser and blend until smooth. Season and serve with fresh crusty bread.

TYPES OF MEAT

Vegetarians can skip this section, but those carnivores out there can now indulge in mental images of fillet steak and Sunday roasts. Students often find themselves unable to afford meat, other than fast-food burgers, on a regular basis, but I would advise against anyone resorting to microwaving next door's cat. Although the price can be beyond the budget of some students, chicken is still relatively inexpensive, and certain cuts of red meats (and that doesn't just include the offal) shouldn't break the bank.

Beef

When choosing a piece of beef it should be a light red colour and slightly elastic, with not too much gristle. But if it contains no gristle it will have a poor flavour.

There are many different cuts of beef, and each is suitable for different methods of cooking:

Roasting
- Topside
- Sirloin
- Fillet
- Ribs
- Rump

Grilling or Frying
- Sirloin
- Fillet
- Rump
- Entrecôte
- Minced

TYPES OF MEAT

Stewing
- Rump
- Brisket
- Flank
- Chuck

Chicken

When buying chicken it should smell fresh and the flesh should be firm. Chicken is very versatile: most parts can be fried, roasted, stewed etc.

Pork

Pork is cheaper than beef and should be a pale red colour. It is important when cooking pork that it is sufficiently done, the danger in eating undercooked pork is that tapeworms can take a fancy to your stomach. The meat should be white, not pink, after cooking.

Roasting
- Ribs
- Loin
- Leg
- Blade-bone

Grilling or Frying
- Chops
- Ribs
- Loin

Lamb

Lamb should be a pinkish red colour, and the bones at the joints should be red.

Roasting	• Shoulder
	• Leg
	• Best end of neck
	• Loin
Grilling or Frying	• Loin chops or cutlets
	• Liver
Stewing	• Loin
	• Leg
	• Breast
	• Liver

MAIN DISHES

This is the most important section of this book, because although there are sections on starters, making cakes etc, my experience as a student tells me there is little time to bake cakes, and the greatest efforts are made when cooking main meals for a whole household. The main meals in this book have an international flavour with the recipes being set out according to country of origin. Some of the recipes can lay claim to belonging to more than one country, so don't moan if you think something is in the wrong place.

The mixture of recipes is diverse, ranging from the standard student dishes like spag bol, chilli con carne, shepherd's pie etc to the lesser known and slightly exotic dishes. None are too complicated, though some are unusual. Don't be put off by the title of a particular recipe – read it through first, as names can be deceptive. And don't worry if your household lacks perhaps one or two of the minor ingredients, since it will probably not matter.

For those who think that any of the recipes are a bit on the expensive side, just remember that most of them could be prepared for the cost of a few pints of beer.

BRITISH

The traditional British fare is often thought of by foreigners as comprising only bangers and mash, jellied eels and early morning fry-ups. This is absolutely true, and I can thoroughly recommend a panful of greasy eggs, bacon and sausages after a hard night studying the local brews.

But things are changing fast, and mangetout could at this rate soon replace mushy peas on the school menus. I have to say, though, that petite portions of nouvelle cuisine are hardly sufficient to feed the average beer belly. With that in mind, I have endeavoured to preserve some vital remnants of our heritage in the following recipes.

BUBBLE AND SQUEAK

This requires scraping the leftovers from the previous day/ week out of the bin-liner, then melting it down to a substance slightly less chewy than industrial glue.

Ingredients

2 tbs of olive oil
Mashed potato
Greens or Brussels sprouts
Egg
**Whatever else has got stuck to
the saucepan overnight**

Fry the mixture until it smells edible, then eat if you dare.

SHEPHERD'S PIE

This popular dish traditionally uses leftover beef from a Sunday roast, but minced beef is an adequate substitute for those not indulging in a roast.

Serves 3 to 4

Ingredients

1 lb (500g) of minced beef
1 onion, peeled and chopped
1 clove of garlic, peeled and finely chopped
1 tin of chopped tomatoes (optional)
1 tbs of tomato purée
1 tsp of mixed herbs
2 tbs of olive oil
5 medium potatoes, peeled
Salt
Pepper

Heat the oil in a largish saucepan, add the onion and garlic, and fry for 3 to 4 minutes. Add the meat and cook for another 10 minutes, then add the other ingredients, except for the potatoes, and simmer for 15 minutes.

While this is simmering, cook the potatoes (test them with a knife – the knife should pass through the potato easily), then mash them with a nob of butter and a bit of milk. Put the meat in an ovenproof dish and cover with the potato, then put under the grill until the potato browns.

SPICY SAUSAGE CASSEROLE

This is ideal for those fed up with boring old sausages and spuds. It is not a traditional English recipe, but I don't know where it originates from, so as I'm English it can stay here.

Serves 4

Ingredients

I pack of pork sausages, cut into pieces
I onion, peeled and chopped
2 cloves of garlic, peeled and finely chopped
I tin of chopped tomatoes
2 tbs of tomato purée
I green pepper, seeded and chopped
½ pint (0.25 litre) of beef stock
2 tsp of chilli powder
I tsp of oregano
2 tbs of olive oil
Salt
Pepper

Heat the oil in a largish saucepan or wok, then gently fry the onion, garlic and chilli powder for about 5 minutes. Then add the sausages and the pepper, and cook for about 10 minutes. Add the tomato purée, beef stock, seasoning, tomatoes and oregano. Simmer for at least 15 minutes then season and serve with rice and peas. Alternatively after cooking the rice and peas add them directly to the casserole and cook for another couple of minutes.

CAULIFLOWER CHEESE

A quick and cheap dish that even a Philosophy student can prepare with ease.

Serves 3 to 4

Ingredients

1 cauliflower
¾ pint (375ml) of milk
1 oz (25g) of cornflour
6 oz (150g) of cheese, grated
1 oz (25g) of butter
Salt
Pepper

Prepare the cheese sauce as outlined in the chapter Dressings and Sauces, (using 4 oz of the cheese) but use ¾ pint (375ml) of milk instead of a pint (0.5 litre). Break the cauliflower into flowerets (clumps) then place in boiling water for about 10 minutes, making sure it is not overcooked.

When the cauliflower is cooked, drain well and place in an ovenproof dish, pour over the cheese sauce, sprinkle on the other 2 oz (50g) of cheese and brown under a hot grill.

TOAD IN THE HOLE

A classic dish with a title that is about as misleading as hedgehog crisps.

Serves 4

Ingredients

4 tbs of vegetable oil
I lb (500g) of sausages
4 oz (100g) of flour
I egg
½ pint (0.25 litre) of milk
Salt

Mix the flour with a pinch of salt, then make a well in the flour and break the egg into it. Add first a little milk to give a smooth texture, then pour in the rest of the milk and beat for a minute or so (the resultant mixture is called batter). Put the sausages in a baking tin with the oil and bake for 10 minutes at Gas Mark 7 (450 °F, 230 °C). Then add the batter and cook for a further 25 minutes or until the batter has risen and is browned.

BEEF STEW

Serves 4

Ingredients

1 lb (500g) of stewing steak
1 onion, peeled and roughly chopped
1 clove of garlic, peeled and chopped
1 ½ oz (40g) of flour
1 pint (0.5 litre) of beef stock
3 carrots, peeled and chopped
1 Bay leaf
2 tbs of olive oil
Salt
Pepper

Cut the meat into 1-inch (2.5cm) pieces and roll them in some of the flour with a little salt and pepper. Heat the oil in a casserole dish then brown the meat on all sides. Remove the meat and set aside. Fry the onion and garlic for 5 minutes in the casserole dish.

Add the rest of the flour to the pan and fry gently. Add the stock and boil until it thickens. Add the bay leaf and carrots, and bake at Gas Mark 4 (350 °F, 180 °C) for 90 minutes.

PORK AND CIDER CASSEROLE

This is a recipe that was achieved by experimentation.

Serves 4

Ingredients

2 tbs of olive oil
I large onion, peeled and chopped
2 cloves of garlic, peeled and finely chopped
I tin of chopped tomatoes
I tbs of tomato purée
2 tsp of mixed herbs
I green pepper, seeded and chopped
I courgette, sliced
4 pork chops
I pint (0.5 litre) of dry cider
I mug of macaroni
½ mug of frozen peas
Salt
Pepper

Heat the oil in a large casserole dish, then fry the onion, garlic and green pepper for about 5 minutes. Then add the pork chops and fry on both sides for a couple of minutes. Add the tomatoes, purée, herbs, courgette, seasoning and cider then bring to the boil.

Simmer for about 40 minutes, adding the macaroni about 10 minutes before serving and the peas about 5 minutes before. Check to see if the macaroni is cooked before serving.

CHICKEN CASSEROLE

Serves 4

Ingredients

4 pieces of chicken (breast, wing or thigh)
½ pint (0.25 litre) of chicken stock
1 tbs of tomato purée
1 onion, peeled and chopped
2 tsp of flour
2 tsp of oregano or mixed herbs
Salt
Pepper

Mix the flour with a little water and then add to the chicken stock.

Add the herbs, onion, tomato purée, salt and pepper. Put the chicken in an ovenproof dish, and pour the stock over it.

Cover the dish with foil and bake in the oven at Gas Mark 4 (350 °F, 180 °C) for 60 minutes. Serve with potatoes and vegetables.

CORNED BEEF HASH

Corned beef suffered a slump in sales when they found companies had been using horse meat as a substitute. However that was many years ago, and it tastes OK to me.

Serves 4

Ingredients

2 tbs of olive oil
1 tin of corned beef
1 large onion, peeled and chopped
Milk
Butter
4 large potatoes
Salt
Pepper

Peel the potatoes and chop them into quarters. Place the potatoes in a saucepan of boiling water and boil for about 20 minutes or until tender. Then drain them and mash with a little milk and butter.

Heat the oil in a large frying pan and fry the onion for about 5 minutes or until it is golden. Open the tin of beef, chop up into small pieces and add to the onion. Heat the beef through and then add the mashed potato. Fry until the potato turns slightly crispy, but not burnt. Season to taste.

MINCED BEEF AND ONIONS

Mince is good value and provides a good basis for many student meals. If you have never tried soya mince, it is not as bad as people make out, so why not give it a try and save yourself a few spondoolies?

Serves 4

Ingredients

2 tbs of olive oil
1 lb (500g) of minced beef
1 onion, peeled and chopped
½ pint (0.25 litre) of gravy
4 oz (100g) of frozen peas
Salt
Pepper

Heat the oil in a frying pan and fry the onion for about 5 minutes. Add the beef, season and cook for another 10 minutes. Mix up the gravy according to the instructions on the packet and add to the mince with the peas. Simmer for about 5 minutes and serve with potatoes.

If you want a bit more flavour try adding a few herbs or even a couple of teaspoons of chilli powder.

COURGETTE AND BACON BAKE

Don't bother with this recipe if you can't stand courgettes.

Serves 4

Ingredients

**2 tbs of olive oil
2 lb (1kg) of courgettes, sliced
4 oz (100g) of bacon, cut into pieces
4 eggs
5 oz (125g) of cheddar cheese, grated
¾ pint (375ml) of milk
1 oz (25g) of butter
Salt
Pepper**

Heat the oil in a large pan. Fry the courgettes for 4 to 5 minutes, then add the bacon and fry for another couple of minutes. Beat the eggs together with the milk, add the cheese and season. Grease a baking dish using the butter and layer the courgettes and bacon until they are used up. Pour the egg and cheese mixture over the top and sprinkle on the rest of the cheese. Bake at Gas Mark 4 (350 °F, 180 °C) for 40 minutes or until golden.

SAUSAGES

The great British banger is one of the country's most famous and highly renowned inventions. After all these years it still provides a cheap, simple and cholesterolly dangerous meal. Sausages come in various types, the most popular variants containing either pork or beef. The price will depend on their fat content – the cheapest might be almost pure tubes of fat. Handmade sausages can still be found at some local butcher shops.

Before cooking your sausages, get a fork and stab them a couple of times. This prevents splitting.

The usual methods for cooking sausages are frying or grilling. For those who want to minimise the relative unhealthiness of the sausage, grilling is the better way to choose.

To fry: heat some oil in a frying pan, and fry the sausages for 15 to 20 minutes. Turn them regularly when cooking to make sure they brown and cook evenly.

To grill: remember to prick the sausages, then grill for about 10 minutes on each side, on a medium heat.

Serve with finger rolls, fried onions and lashings of ketchup.

MEATBALLS

Serves 4

Ingredients

2 tbs of olive oil
I lb (500g) of minced beef
I egg, beaten
I onion, peeled and finely chopped
3 slices of bread
I tbs of freshly chopped parsley
I tsp of smooth French mustard
I tsp of chilli powder
Salt
Pepper

Remove the crusts from the bread, then tear into minuscule pieces. Those with a blender can give them a whizz for a few secs.

Mix the breadcrumbs, mince, parsley, chilli powder, mustard, beaten egg, onion and seasoning together and mould into balls.

Then heat the oil in a frying pan and fry your balls evenly for about 10 to 15 minutes, turning regularly. Don't make the balls too big or they will not cook in the middle.

LAMB AND LEEK CASSEROLE

Serves 4

Ingredients

2 tbs of olive oil
4 lamb chops
1 onion, peeled and sliced
2 leeks, sliced
½ lb (250g) of carrots, peeled and chopped
4 oz (100g) of peas
1 pint (0.5 litre) of beef/vegetable stock
Salt
Pepper

Heat the oil in a frying pan then fry the chops for a couple of minutes on each side. Then add the onion, carrots and leek, and fry for a few more minutes.

Transfer into a casserole dish, season, and pour the stock over. Put a lid on the dish and place in the oven at Gas Mark 4 (350 °F, 180 °C) for about 1 hour. Add the peas about 15 minutes before serving.

TUNA MORNAY

Serves 4

Ingredients

**4 hard-boiled eggs
I large tin of tuna
6 tomatoes, sliced
½ pint (0.25 litre) of white sauce or cheese sauce
I oz (25g) of cheese, grated
Chopped parsley or watercress
Salt
Pepper**

Cut the eggs in half, lengthways. Mix the yolks with the tuna. Place the sliced tomatoes in a greased oven dish, then place the whites of the eggs on the tomatoes.

Spoon the mixture of tuna and yolk onto the egg whites. Make the sauce according to the packet instructions or for cheese sauce follow the recipe given in the chapter Dressings and Sauces, and pour the sauce over the mixture while it is hot. Season, then sprinkle with grated cheese.

Place in a moderate oven at Gas Mark 6 (425 °F, 220 °C) for about 20 minutes until lightly browned. Garnish with parsley or watercress.

HOT CHICKEN

Serves 4

Ingredients

4 pieces of chicken
1 onion, peeled and chopped
1 green pepper, seeded and chopped
2 tbs of olive oil
1 tin of chopped tomatoes
3 tsp of chilli powder
Salt
Pepper

Heat the oil in a large saucepan and fry the onions for 3 to 4 minutes, then add the chilli powder, salt and pepper. Cook for another couple of minutes.

Add the chicken and the pepper and cook for about 10 minutes. Then add the tomatoes and simmer for 40 minutes, adding a little water if the sauce begins to burn. Serve with rice.

ROAST DINNERS

The traditional Sunday roast hasn't yet died out in our house, although it is more often served in the evening than at lunchtime. Those sharing a house will find it is good to make the effort to have a roast, as it makes a pleasant change from all the rushed meals that are grabbed between lectures during the rest of the week.

Remember that when using the oven, it should be switched on 20 minutes before the joint is put in to heat it up to the correct temperature.

ROAST BEEF

*Serves 2 to 20 (depending on whether you
have a small joint or a whole cow)*

Ingredients

**1 joint of beef
¼ pint (125ml) of vegetable oil
Gravy
Salt
Pepper**

Before throwing away the packaging for your joint, note how much it weighs. Allow 20 minutes cooking time per pound, plus 20 minutes on top, all at Gas Mark 7 (450 °F, 230 °C). This will allow for cooking the meat 'English style', i.e. with not too much blood seeping out. If you prefer it 'rare', cook for about 15 minutes less.

Put the joint in a roasting tin and pour the oil over the top and the sides. Season heavily with the salt and pepper, and stick in the oven.

The joint must be 'basted' – that means spooning the oil in the tin over the top of the meat to stop it from drying out. Do this two or three times during cooking.

When the meat is cooked, carve the joint and serve with fresh vegetables. Gravy can be made from the juices in the roasting tin.

ROAST PORK

This must be cooked for a little longer than beef, as it is essential that pork is well cooked. Prepare in the same method as the beef but cook for 25 minutes per pound plus 25 minutes over, on the same oven setting. Baste the joint every 20 minutes. If you like garlic try sticking pieces of garlic in the joint before cooking.

ROAST LAMB

Lamb can be quite expensive but has a wonderful flavour that makes it worth splashing out on occasionally.

Prepare in the same method as the beef and cook for 20 minutes per pound and 20 minutes extra on the same oven setting. Baste every 20 minutes. Add some sprigs of rosemary for extra flavour.

ROAST CHICKEN

It is important not to overcook chicken as it loses all its flavour and is harder to carve.

Place the chicken in a baking tin with ¼ (125ml) pint of oil and season with plenty of black pepper and bake for 15 to 20 minutes per pound plus 20 minutes at Gas Mark 6 (425 °F, 220 °C).

ROAST POTATOES

Peel the potatoes and cut them in half or even quarters if they are large. Boil them for 5 minutes in slightly salted water. Drain using a colander, then return them to the saucepan and shake them around to rough up the edges. This will help them to become nice and crisp. Place them in the baking tray with the joint and baste them with the fat. Season with salt and pepper. Allow at least 50 to 60 minutes for them to cook.

ITALIAN

For those who think of Italy only as the vague backdrop to *The Merchant of Venice* laboriously studied at school, think again. You haven't lived until you have discovered the wonders of Italy and its cuisine.

Choosing Pasta

Pasta is probably one of the most widely used ingredients in Italian cooking and, like the French, Italians are not hesitant in the use of garlic and fresh herbs. The advantage of cooking with pasta is that there is almost no limit to what you can do with it. Obviously there are set rules and standard recipes, but personal experimentation is important and fun. Fresh pasta (as a friend commented, 'that soggy stuff in a packet') is now quite common, especially in the large supermarkets, although those on a grant will find it cheaper to use the dried variety.

After choosing between fresh and dried pasta there is also the decision as to what type to use. Pasta comes in a wide range of shapes and sizes, perhaps the most common being spaghetti. It can also be found in the shape of shells, quills, ribbons and twists, to name but a few. For those who have not outgrown tinned pasta you might be lucky enough to get space invaders, but I don't think that the Italians would approve.

Cooking Pasta

Correct cooking of the pasta is essential. After the water has boiled add a pinch of salt. Long pasta like spaghetti should be eased gently into a pan making sure that it is not broken.

Adding a couple of drops of olive oil can prevent sticking. The pasta should be cooked with the lid off, and stirred occasionally.

Normally, dried pasta requires 8 to 10 minutes in boiling water. Someone once told me that the best way to see if it is cooked is to throw a piece on the wall. If it sticks, it's ready. Apart from making a mess on your wall this is not the most reliable way to test the pasta. While it should have some 'bite' to it (al dente), make sure that the pasta is not too undercooked, as this could result in indigestion (otherwise known as 'gut rot').

If you are cooking fresh pasta it normally only requires 2 or 3 minutes, so watch it carefully. If you overcook your pasta it will stick together and will taste very doughy.

The secret of getting a wonderful tasting sauce is to **reduce** it. This entails simmering the sauce until the liquid thickens and its volume reduces. When this happens the flavours are enhanced. If you have time, let the sauce simmer for at least 20 minutes.

BASIC TOMATO SAUCE

Serves 3 to 4

Ingredients

**2 tbs of olive oil
1 large onion, peeled and chopped
2 cloves of garlic, peeled and finely chopped
1 tin of chopped tomatoes
1 tbs of tomato purée
6 fresh basil leaves or 1 tsp of dried oregano
Salt
Pepper**

Heat the oil in a saucepan, then add the chopped onion and garlic and fry gently for 3 to 4 minutes. When these have softened, add the tomatoes, purée, herbs, salt and pepper. Cook for another 20 minutes until they have been reduced.

Serve with a pasta of your choice.

TOMATO AND TUNA SAUCE

This is one of my most used recipes when studying.

Serves 4

Ingredients

2 tbs of olive oil
I medium onion, peeled and chopped
I clove of garlic, peeled and finely chopped
I tin of chopped tomatoes
I tbs of tomato purée
I tin of tuna
I tsp of oregano
I tsp of brown sugar
Salt
Pepper

Heat the oil in a medium-sized saucepan and fry the onion and garlic for about 5 minutes. Then add the tomatoes, purée, oregano, salt, pepper and sugar. Simmer for about 15 minutes or until the sauce has been reduced. Add the tuna and cook for a further 5 minutes. Serve with a pasta of your choice and grated parmesan if you have any.

SPAGHETTI BOLOGNESE

Most students have probably tried preparing this classic Italian dish at some point. There are many variations of the recipe, this is my preferred one.

Serves 4

Ingredients

2 tbs of olive oil
1 lb (500g) of minced beef
1 onion, peeled and chopped
1 tin of chopped tomatoes
4 oz (100g) of mushrooms, washed and sliced
2 cloves of garlic, peeled and finely chopped
1 carrot, peeled and grated
2 rashers of bacon, cut into small pieces
1 large glass of red wine (optional)
1 tbs of tomato purée
¾ pint (375ml) of beef stock
Salt
Pepper

Heat the oil in a large saucepan, then add the onion and garlic, and fry gently for 5 minutes, being careful not to burn them. Add the minced beef and continue frying for a further 10 minutes. Then add the other remaining ingredients.

After your sauce has reduced, which takes around 20 minutes, serve with a pasta of your choice – it doesn't have to be spaghetti – and a sprinkling of parmesan on top.

TOMATO AND HAM PASTA SAUCE

Serves 4

Ingredients

2 tbs of olive oil
1 tin of chopped tomatoes
1 onion, peeled and chopped
4 slices of ham, cut into strips
2 cloves of garlic, peeled and finely chopped
1 tbs of tomato purée
1 glass of red wine (optional)
2 tsp of oregano/mixed herbs
Salt
Pepper

Heat the oil in a saucepan and fry the onion and garlic for about 5 minutes. Then add the other ingredients and simmer for 20 minutes. Serve with a pasta of your choice, topped with parmesan or cheddar cheese.

CARBONARA

I'm not sure if this is the traditional recipe for the dish, but it tastes good to me.

Serves 3 to 4

Ingredients

2 tbs of olive oil
2 mugs of pasta quills/shells
1 clove of garlic, peeled and finely chopped
6 rashers of streaky bacon, cut into small pieces
3 egg yolks, beaten
2 oz (50g) of parmesan cheese, grated
3 tbs single cream
Salt
Pepper

Boil the pasta in a saucepan for about 12 minutes, or according to the instruction on the packet. 5 minutes before the pasta is cooked, fry the bacon and garlic in the oil for 4 to 5 minutes. When the pasta is cooked, drain, and add to the bacon. Then add the cheese, egg, cream and seasoning. Heat until the egg has cooked, stirring constantly (this should take just a couple of minutes), then serve immediately with more black pepper.

PASTA WITH COURGETTE AND BACON SAUCE

If you don't have any bacon, slices of ham could be used.

Serves 4

Ingredients

2 tbs of olive oil
1 onion, peeled and chopped
1 clove of garlic, peeled and finely chopped
1 tin of chopped tomatoes
1 tbs of tomato purée
2 rashers of bacon, cut into strips
2 courgettes, thinly sliced
2 tsp of oregano
Salt
Pepper

Heat the oil in a large saucepan, then add the onion and garlic. Fry for about 3 or 4 minutes, then add the bacon and courgettes. Continue cooking for another 5 minutes, but don't have the heat up too high otherwise the onion will start to burn. A tablespoon of water can be added to help the cooking and to prevent any burning.

When the courgettes have softened add the tomatoes, purée, seasoning and herbs. Simmer the sauce for at least 15 to 20 minutes then serve with pasta and parmesan or grated cheddar on top.

LASAGNE

This is one of everybody's favourite Italian dishes. See the vegetarian section for an alternative recipe.

Serves 4

Ingredients

2 tbs of oil
1 large onion, peeled and chopped
2 cloves of garlic, peeled and finely chopped
1 lb (500g) of minced beef
1 tin of chopped tomatoes
¼ pint (125ml) of beef stock
2 tbs of tomato purée
1 packet of lasagne (no pre-cooking required type)
2 tsp of oregano
Salt
Pepper

For the sauce:

1 oz (25g) of butter
2 oz (50g) of flour
1 pint (0.5 litre) of milk
6 oz (150g) of cheese, grated

After heating the oil in a saucepan, add the onion and garlic and cook for 5 minutes. Add the mince and cook thoroughly. Then add the tomatoes, oregano, beef stock, tomato purée and seasoning. After bringing to the boil, an optional simmering for 15 to 20 minutes will improve the flavour.

While the meat sauce is reducing, prepare the cheese sauce. Melt the butter in a saucepan and then add the flour, stirring constantly. Remove from the heat and add the milk in stages. If the milk is added in one go, you end up with lumps in the sauce. After adding the milk, bring to the boil and add the cheese, saving a bit for the top. Then simmer for 3 or 4 minutes; the sauce should now begin to thicken.

OK, so your sauce has not thickened: don't panic! Try adding a bit more flour, but sieve it first if you can. Lumpiness can be rectified by pouring the mixture through a sieve.

Find a shallow baking dish and grease it, then add a layer of meat sauce followed by a layer of lasagne, followed by a layer of cheese sauce. Continue this formation until you have used up your mixtures, making sure you finish with the cheese sauce. As well as sprinkling cheese on top, fresh tomato slices can be added.

Bake on the middle shelf of a preheated oven at Gas Mark 6 (425 °F, 220 °C) for 30 to 40 minutes.

PASTA WITH SAUSAGE

It might seem like an unusual combination but it works well.

Serves 4

Ingredients

4 thick spicy sausages
14 oz (350g) of tagliatelle
1 oz (25g) of butter
2 tbs of olive oil
2 oz (50g) of finely grated parmesan
1 clove of garlic, peeled and crushed
1 courgette
2 tbs of fresh basil
2 tbs of fresh chives
2 tbs of fresh parsley
Salt
Pepper

Grill or fry the sausages until cooked then cut into slices. Cook the pasta with a drop of olive oil added to the water to stop it sticking together. Cut the courgette into thin strips so that they look like matchsticks and fry in a little olive oil with the garlic for a couple of minutes. Finely chop the herbs. When the pasta is cooked, drain and return to the pan. Throw in the cheese, herbs, sausage and butter, mix thoroughly and season. If the cheese has not melted return to the heat for a minute.

MACARONI CHEESE WITH TOMATO

This is another of my favourite recipes. If you don't have any macaroni try using pasta shells.

Serves 4

Ingredients

4 oz (100g) of macaroni
6 oz (150g) of cheddar cheese, grated
2 large tomatoes, sliced
¾ pint (375ml) of milk
1 oz (25g) of flour or cornflour
1 oz (25g) of butter
Salt
Pepper

Melt the butter in a saucepan and mix in the flour, then gradually add the milk, stirring constantly to avoid lumps. Bring to the boil, add the cheese, then leave to simmer for 3 to 4 minutes.

Now cook the macaroni according to the instructions on the packet. When this is done, drain and mix with the cheese sauce. Put into a baking dish, top with sliced tomatoes and more cheese, season, and then grill until browned.

POTATO AND TOMATO CAKE

Serves 4

Ingredients

**2 tbs of olive oil
2 lb (1kg) of 'old' potatoes
1 tin of chopped tomatoes
1 onion, peeled and finely chopped
Salt
Pepper**

Heat the oil in a pan and fry the onion gently for 10 minutes then add the tomatoes, salt and pepper. Keep the heat low and simmer for about 20 minutes so the sauce reduces to a thick liquid.

Whilst the sauce is reducing, boil the potatoes until they are soft enough to mash. Gradually mix the sauce with the mashed potatoes.

When all the sauce is added, spoon the mixture out onto a serving plate and mould into the shape of a cake. Eat hot or cold.

PIZZA

Huge scope for variety here, both in toppings and bases. The easiest to make is the French bread pizza, because the base is simply a sliced baguette. Dough bases can be bought ready-made, but they cost more than French sticks or homemade doughs.

PIZZA MARGHERITA

This is the basic pizza. If you want to design your own, use this and add your own toppings.

Serves 1

Ingredients

1 stick of French bread
Ragu/tomato purée
1 tsp of olive oil
1 oz (25g) of grated cheese
Pinch of oregano
Pepper

Slice the French stick in half and spread some tomato purée on top. A thin layer will do – if you put too much on your pizza will become soggy. Place the cheese on top, season, add the herbs and pour on the oil. Bake in the oven until the cheese turns a golden brown colour. It should take roughly 15 minutes at Gas Mark 7 (450 °F, 230 °C).

PIZZA ROMA

Serves 1

Ingredients

1 stick of French bread
Ragu/tomato purée
1 tsp of oil
1 oz (25g) of cheese, grated
2 oz (50g) of tuna
2 to 3 onion rings
Pinch of oregano
Pepper

Spread some tomato purée on the bread. Place the tuna on first, then the onion rings and finally the cheese. Season, add the oregano and oil and cook as for the previous recipe.

ITALIAN

There is almost no limit to what you can put on a pizza. Here is a list of suggested toppings that can be used as a basis for designing your own.

- Ham
- Pepperoni
- Tuna
- Mushrooms
- Onions
- Green peppers
- Red peppers
- Fresh tomatoes
- Spinach
- Egg
- Olives
- Sultanas
- Leeks
- Capers
- Anchovies
- Hot green chilli peppers
- Pineapple
- Sweetcorn
- Exotic cheeses

CHICKEN RISOTTO

Serves 4

Ingredients

1 oz (25g) of butter
1 onion, peeled and chopped
1 clove of garlic, peeled and finely chopped
3 oz (75g) of chicken, cut into pieces
8 oz (200g) of aborio rice
2 oz (50g) of mushrooms, sliced
1 pint (0.5 litre) of chicken stock
Salt
Pepper

Heat the butter in a large saucepan and fry the chicken pieces for 5 minutes, then remove from the pan and put them in a bowl.

Fry the onion and garlic for 3 to 4 minutes. Put the rice in a sieve and wash under cold water to remove the starch. Then add the rice to the onions and fry gently for a couple more minutes.

Prepare the stock using boiling water, then add to the rice a little at a time. Stir whilst adding the stock. Let the rice simmer gently until the stock is all absorbed and the rice is cooked. This should take about 20 minutes. Season.

When the rice is cooked add the chicken and mushrooms and cook for a minute or so, to heat them through.

FRENCH

The French like to think of themselves as producing the best lovers, the finest wines, and the Citroen 2CV. In spite of this, the French can produce food which is extremely palatable, especially when washed down with a few litres of Beaujolais.

CHICKEN IN BEER

The temptation is always to leave out the chicken from this recipe, but aim for restraint.

Serves 4

Ingredients

2 tbs of olive oil
4 chicken pieces
I onion, peeled and chopped
3 carrots, peeled and chopped
I leek, sliced
4 oz (100g) of mushrooms, sliced
I large can of your favourite lager/ale
Salt
Pepper

Heat the oil in a casserole dish, then fry the onion for 3 to 4 minutes. Add the chicken and fry for another 10 minutes. Chuck the rest of the ingredients in the dish then stick in the oven for 1 hour at Gas Mark 5 (400 °F, 200 °C).

Then drink the rest of the beer, taking care not to get so drunk that you forget to take the chicken out of the oven.

PORK PROVENÇAL

This recipe is based on one of the fine offerings
of Hotel du Commerce, Castellane.

Serves 4

Ingredients

2 tbs of olive oil
4 pork chops
I onion, peeled and chopped
I clove of garlic, peeled and finely chopped
I tin of chopped tomatoes
I red pepper, seeded and finely chopped
2 tsp of herbes de Provence or mixed herbs
I courgette, finely chopped
4 slices of cheddar cheese
Salt
Pepper

Heat the oil in a saucepan. Fry the onion and garlic in the oil for about 5 minutes. When these have cooked, add the tomatoes, red pepper, courgette, herbs and seasoning. Let the sauce simmer for 20 minutes. After 10 minutes, grill the pork on foil, turning occasionally, and when it is nearly cooked put some sauce and the slices of cheese on the pork and grill until the cheese begins to melt.

Note that thinner pork chops will take less cooking time. Serve with potatoes and fresh vegetables and the rest of the sauce.

LEMON CHICKEN

This recipe is a refreshing change to the more common ways of presenting chicken.

Serves 2

Ingredients

2 tbs of olive oil
2 chicken breasts
Juice of 1 lemon
Salt
Pepper

Cut the chicken into small pieces (this allows the lemon to flavour a larger area). Heat the oil in large frying pan then add the chicken, lemon juice and seasoning. Fry for 5 minutes, or until the chicken is cooked all the way through, adding more lemon juice before serving, if required.

Serve with a salad and pitta or French bread.

CHICKEN IN WINE

This recipe uses only one glass of wine, so if you have a bit left over from last night's booze-up, use that.

Serves 4

Ingredients

4 chicken pieces
I large glass of red or white wine
2 onions, peeled and chopped
½ pint (0.25 litre) of vegetable stock
2 tbs of flour
2 tbs of olive oil
Salt
Pepper

Put the flour in a dish and roll the chicken pieces in it until they are evenly covered. Heat the oil in a large saucepan then fry the onions for 5 minutes or until they are golden. Then fry the chicken pieces for another 5 minutes. Add the stock, onions, seasoning and, of course, the wine, and simmer for 45 minutes.

QUICHE

For this recipe an 8-inch (20cm) flan dish and a rolling pin are needed.

Once the basic technique of making a quiche is mastered, limitless combinations of this classic French dish can be produced. Many people are put off preparing a quiche because it involves making pastry, but it is not as hard as it sounds.

SHORT CRUST PASTRY

Ingredients for pastry

**8 oz (200g) of plain flour
4 oz (100g) of butter
3 tbs of water
Pinch of salt**

This is perhaps one of the only times when I would make the effort to sieve the flour and salt, but don't worry if you don't possess such an implement. After sieving the flour and the salt add the butter. It is easier to rub in if the fat is cut into little cubes.

The term 'rubbing in' is the procedure in which, using the fingertips, the flour and the fat are combined to produce a mixture the consistency of fine breadcrumbs.

After rubbing in, add some water a little at a time. The water is needed to bind the mixture together, but be careful not to add so much as to make the pastry become sticky.

Mould the pastry into a ball then roll out on a floured board or very clean floured work surface. Also sprinkle a coating of flour onto the rolling pin. The flour is used to stop the pastry from sticking to the board and the pin.

Roll the pastry so that its area is big enough to cover the flan dish, then carefully place the pastry over the dish and mould it in the shape of the dish. Remove the edge of the overlapping pastry by running a knife along the rim of dish.

The next stage is to make the filling of the quiche.

CHEESE AND ONION QUICHE

A delicious quiche filling. Nicer than a tooth filling, anyway.

Ingredients for filling

I tbs of olive oil
4 eggs
½ pint (0.25 litre) of milk
4 oz (100g) of cheddar cheese, grated
I onion, peeled and chopped
Salt
Pepper

Heat the oil in a frying pan, then lightly fry the onion for a couple of minutes. Place the onion on the bottom of the pastry case. Beat the eggs together, add the milk, season and beat again. Pour over the onion, sprinkle the cheese on top, then bake in a hot oven at Gas Mark 6 (425 °F, 220 °C), for 25 minutes or until the filling is cooked.

QUICHE LORRAINE

The most famous quiche of all has to be the Lorraine. Its name derives from its region of origin, and it is delicious eaten hot or cold. Unfortunately I have had to corrupt this recipe slightly by cutting out the cream as this makes it rather expensive for students. But if you are feeling flush then half the milk can be substituted for single cream: it's well worth it.

Serves 4

Ingredients for filling

4 eggs
½ pint (0.25 litre) of milk
4 oz (100g) of bacon
2 oz (50g) of cheese (optional)
Salt
Pepper

Cut the bacon into small pieces, then fry lightly for a couple of minutes and place on the bottom of the pastry base. Beat the eggs together, add the milk, season and beat again.

Pour over the bacon, sprinkle the cheese on top if required and bake in a hot oven at Gas Mark 6 (425 °F, 220 °C), for 25 minutes or until the filling has set.

CHICKEN WITH MUSHROOMS AND PEPPERS

Serves 4

Ingredients

2 tbs of olive oil
4 chicken pieces (breast, leg, thigh etc)
I green pepper, seeded and sliced into rings
4 oz (100g) of mushrooms, washed and sliced
I pint (0.5 litre) of chicken stock
I onion, peeled and chopped
Salt
Pepper

Heat the oil in a medium-sized saucepan, then fry the onion and chicken for about 5 minutes.

Add the mushrooms, pepper and seasoning and continue frying for another 10 minutes. Pour the chicken stock over the top and simmer for 30 minutes. Serve with potatoes or rice.

ORIENTAL

Too often oriental cuisine is thought of as 'flied lice' and a bit of chop suey served in a foil carton. This is not the true taste of the Orient, but unfortunately it is not always possible to find a decent and unclichéd menu. With the availability of fresh oriental produce in most supermarkets, many people have taken to home experimentation.

We'll just stick to home cooking, though.

RED SNAPPER WITH GINGER

Serves 1 to 2, depending on size of fish

Ingredients

**1 red snapper, cleaned
1 clove of garlic, peeled and finely chopped
2 tsp of soy sauce
Juice of 1 lime
1 oz (25g) of fresh ginger, peeled and thinly sliced**

Place the fish on a piece of tin foil. Mix the lime juice, soy sauce, garlic and ginger together and pour over the fish. Seal the fish up in the foil and bake in the oven for 40 minutes at Gas Mark 5 (400 °F, 200 °C).

STIR-FRY

Those fortunate enough to possess a wok will find oriental cooking a lot easier than those stuck with the indignity of a frying pan. If you do have to use a frying pan use the biggest one you have. The wok is one of my most used kitchen accessories – its use does not have to be confined to oriental cooking alone.

It is up to you what to put in a stir-fry, though it is often a good way of using up any spare vegetables that are lurking in the back of your cupboard and are undergoing a metamorphosis into a different life form.

VEGETABLE STIR-FRY

Serves 4

Ingredients

2 tbs of olive oil
1 red pepper, seeded and chopped
1 onion, peeled and chopped
1 green pepper, seeded and chopped
1 carrot, peeled and cut into thin strips
1 clove of garlic, peeled and finely chopped
1 tin of bamboo shoots
1 tin of water chestnuts
1 pack of fresh beansprouts
2 tbs of soy sauce
Salt
Pepper

Pour the oil into your wok or frying pan, then when the oil is hot, i.e. when it is smoking (try not to set fire to the kitchen in the process), add the onion and garlic, and fry for 5 minutes. If you are using water chestnuts, cook these first as they take the longest to cook, and are nicer when they are slightly crispy. Then add the soy sauce, seasoning and other vegetables except for the beansprouts.

After frying the vegetables for about 5 to 10 minutes, add the beansprouts and cook for a couple more minutes. It is important to keep the beansprouts firm. Serve with rice.

PORK STIR-FRY

Serves 2

Ingredients

2 tbs of olive oil
½ lb (250g) of diced pork
I green pepper, seeded and chopped
I onion, peeled and chopped
2 tsp of chilli powder
I clove of garlic, peeled and sliced
I tbs of soy sauce

Heat the oil in a large frying pan or wok, then fry the onion and the garlic for about 3 to 4 minutes. Add the pepper, soy sauce, chilli powder and the pork and fry until the pork is cooked. This should take about 10 minutes, depending on the size of the meat pieces. Serve with rice.

COCONUT AND CHICKEN SOUP

This recipe is based on a dish that I had in a restaurant on a remote island in Thailand. I had some of the best meals in my life in MaMa's, even though the restaurant was hardly more than a tin shack.

Serves 4

Ingredients

2 tbs of olive oil
3 chicken breasts
3 oz (75g) of soluble coconut
2 oz (50g) of fresh ginger
I tsp of flour
4 tbs of cream (optional)
Pinch of curry powder
Salt
Pepper

Remove the skin from the chicken, then chop into bite-sized pieces. Heat the oil in a large saucepan, and fry the chicken for about 5 minutes, turning frequently to stop it sticking to the pan.

Using a sharp knife remove the outer layer of the ginger and then slice it into thin pieces. Don't make the pieces too small as they shouldn't be eaten. Add the ginger, curry powder, flour and seasoning to the chicken.

Dissolve the coconut in water – it is easier if the water is hot. Add the coconut to the other ingredients, bring to the boil, then simmer for 15 to 20 minutes. The cream should be added 5 minutes before serving.

Serve the soup with a side order of rice.

INDIAN

Indian cuisine is probably the most fascinating area of cooking I have yet come across. I have only made one brief trip to India, but it's a country I will never forget and to which I am most keen to return. I would like to have had more time to learn about the different regional culinary influences, as Indian cuisine is richly diverse in this way.

Indian cooking for most people is simplified by using ready-prepared curry powders. This, although it will undoubtedly produce a curry, will not represent the true flavour of India. Purists will know that the secret of Indian gastronomy is in the use of a vast combination of different spices and flavourings. I am not saying you can't make a good curry without these spices, but they certainly make a difference to the taste.

It is unfortunate that some people seem to just try and produce the hottest curry they can by shovelling in a tin of curry powder and a dozen chillies, so they can impress their friends with their machismo. The idea of curry is to produce a combination of flavours and tastes that harmonise together, not to produce a vile discord and numb your mouth into oblivion. The recipes in this section are fairly standard and do not require the use of anything too difficult to obtain.

If you share my passion for Indian food it is worthwhile reading some specialist Indian cookbooks. They will explain about the wide variety of spices available, and may have more exciting and original recipes than I can offer.

VEGETABLE CURRY

Curry is one dish that most students are familiar with, though not normally when in a state of complete consciousness. A four-pack, a video and a vindaloo often make for an entertaining night in.
Half an hour in the kitchen could yield a curry that would last you and your mates a few days and still be cheaper than buying from the local Taj. There are literally thousands of different recipes for curry, but a vegetable curry is both amazingly cheap and as suited for freezing as the South Pole. So why not make a bit extra and save it for when the money runs out mid-term?

Serves 4

Ingredients

4 potatoes, diced into 1-inch (2.5cm) cubes
1 leek, sliced
1 tin of chopped tomatoes
2 courgettes, sliced
1 onion, peeled and chopped
2 cloves of garlic, peeled and finely chopped
1 small pot of natural yoghurt
1 tbs of madras curry powder
1 dried red chilli
½ pint (0.25 litre) of beef stock
Any spare vegetables
2 tbs of olive oil
1 to 2 tbs of water
Salt
Pepper

Heat the oil in a large saucepan then fry the onion, garlic and curry powder for 5 minutes or until the onion has softened. Then add the other ingredients, except the yoghurt. Season, then bring to the boil, and simmer for 40 minutes or more. Add the yoghurt 5 minutes before serving.

Whilst the curry is simmering taste it to see if it is to the strength required. If it is not hot enough for your asbestos-lined mouth just add more curry powder. Serve with rice – if you can afford it use pilau or basmati rice.

CUCUMBER RAITA

If the roof of your mouth is feeling like a furnace, this might help. Cucumber raita is a side dish that is very refreshing and simple to prepare.

Serves 2 to 4

Ingredients

½ cucumber, peeled and chopped into pieces
I small pot of natural yoghurt
I tbs of olive oil
I tbs of freshly chopped mint
Salt
Pepper

Mix the cucumber, yoghurt and mint together in a bowl, pour the oil on top, and season.

CHICKEN CURRY

Serves 4

Ingredients

2 tbs of olive oil
4 chicken pieces
2 onions, peeled and chopped
2 cloves of garlic, peeled and finely chopped
3 tsp of curry powder
1 tsp of garam masala
2 fresh green chilli peppers, chopped into rings
1 tin of chopped tomatoes
3 whole green cardamom pods
2 tbs of freshly chopped coriander
1 small pot of natural yoghurt
1 to 2 tbs of water
Salt
Pepper

Heat the oil in a large saucepan, then fry the onions and garlic gently for 5 minutes or until they have softened.

Add the curry powder, garam masala and chillies, and fry for a couple more minutes. Add the chicken and water and fry for 5 minutes. Season. After this the other ingredients can be added, apart from the yoghurt, which is added 5 minutes before serving. Simmer for 30 to 40 minutes, then serve with rice.

CURRIED EGGS

Serves 4

Ingredients

4 eggs
I onion, peeled and finely chopped
4 tomatoes, finely chopped
3 tsp of curry powder
¼ pint (125ml) of water
2 tsp of tomato purée
I small pot of natural yoghurt
I oz (25g) of butter
Salt
Pepper

Place the eggs in a saucepan with some water and boil for 8 minutes. While the eggs are boiling put the butter in a frying pan and fry the onions with the curry powder for 5 minutes. Then stir in the tomatoes, tomato purée, salt, pepper, flour and the water. Bring to the boil, then simmer for 10 to 15 minutes. Peel the eggs then cut them in half and add them to the curry with the yoghurt. Simmer for another 5 minutes then serve with rice.

INDIAN

CHICKEN TANDOORI

Making your own tandoori will cost much less than buying from a takeaway or even a supermarket. This recipe can be eaten cold with salad.

Serves 4

Ingredients

**4 chicken pieces (breast, thigh or wing)
1 tbs of tandoori powder
1 clove of garlic, peeled and finely chopped
½ pint (0.25 litre) of plain unsweetened
natural yoghurt**

Remove the skin from the chicken and make some small incisions in the flesh with a sharp knife – this is to allow the marinade to penetrate deep into the chicken.

Mix the garlic, tandoori powder and yoghurt together, then rub some of the mixture into the incisions. Leave the chicken in the marinade for at least 3 hours, turning occasionally. The longer it is left the more flavour it will gain.

Cook under a medium-heat grill for about 20 minutes, spooning on some more marinade at the same time. Turn the chicken over every few minutes to prevent burning.

Serve hot or cold.

GREEK

Copious quantities of lager in the pub, perhaps a bit of a dance, then to finish off the perfect evening a kebab with extra chilli sauce – all you need for a memorable night out.

SHISH KEBAB

Serves 4

Ingredients

¾ lb (375g) of lamb, cut into small cubes
1 pot of natural yoghurt
Juice of 1 lemon
1 tbs of olive oil
Fresh rosemary
Salt
Pepper

Prepare this meal well in advance, as the lamb has to marinate for at least a couple of hours in order to obtain its full flavour. Put the lamb in a bowl with the yoghurt, lemon juice, olive oil and seasoning. Stir well, then put the bowl in the fridge for a couple of hours, making sure the lamb is evenly coated in the marinade.

When ready to be cooked, divide the meat onto 4 skewers, place on the grill pan with the rosemary and grill for 10 to 15 minutes, turning the kebabs occasionally so they cook evenly. If there is any spare marinade use it to flavour the meat while it is being grilled.

Serve with salad and pitta bread.

MOUSSAKA

Serves 4

Ingredients

1 large aubergine, sliced
2 onions, peeled and chopped
1 tin of chopped tomatoes
1 tbs of tomato purée
1 clove of garlic, crushed and finely chopped
1 lb (500g) of minced beef or lamb
2 tbs of olive oil
1 oz (25g) of butter
1 oz (25g) of flour
¾ pint (375ml) of milk
4 oz (100g) of cheese, grated
Salt
Pepper

Heat a tablespoon of oil in a frying pan and fry the aubergines until they are soft. Then place on a piece of kitchen towel to absorb the fat. Put some more oil in the frying pan if needed and fry the onions, garlic and meat. After about 10 minutes season, and add the tomatoes and purée.

Grease a casserole dish with either butter or oil, and fill it with alternate layers of aubergine and meat, finishing with a layer of aubergine.

To make the cheese sauce, melt the butter in a saucepan, add the flour, and mix together. Remove from the heat, and very gradually add the milk. Boil until the sauce thickens, then remove from the heat and add 3 oz (75g) of the cheese. Pour the cheese sauce over the top of the aubergine, and sprinkle on the rest of the cheese. Bake for 40 minutes at Gas Mark 5 (400 °F, 200 °C). Season to taste.

HUNGARIAN

GOULASH

This dish traditionally uses veal, but beef is often substituted due to the controversy surrounding the methods by which veal is produced.

Serves 4

Ingredients

2 tbs of olive oil
1 large onion, peeled and chopped
1 lb (500g) of potatoes, peeled and sliced
1 clove of garlic, peeled and finely chopped
1 lb (500g) of cubed stewing beef
1 red pepper, seeded and chopped
1 green pepper, seeded and chopped
½ tsp of caraway seeds
1 tbs of paprika
1 tsp of mixed herbs
1 beef stock cube
¾ pint (375ml) of boiling water
4 oz (100g) of sliced mushrooms
1 tin of chopped tomatoes
¼ pint (125ml) of soured cream (optional)
Salt
Pepper

STUDENT GRUB

Heat the oil in a casserole dish or a large saucepan, then fry the onion and garlic for a couple of minutes. Add the meat, peppers, tomatoes, paprika, caraway seeds, herbs, salt and pepper, and cook for about 5 minutes.

Dissolve the stock cube in the boiling water and add to the above. Simmer for about 40 minutes, then add the potatoes and cook for another 40 minutes. After about 30 minutes add the mushrooms. If they are added any earlier they will be overcooked and go mushy.

Before serving add the soured cream, if required.

CHICKEN PAPRIKA

Serves 4

Ingredients

4 chicken portions, skinned
1 clove of garlic, peeled and finely chopped
2 large onions, peeled and chopped
2 tbs of olive oil
¼ pint (125 ml) of soured cream
1 tbs of paprika
¼ pint (125ml) of chicken stock
Salt
Pepper

Heat the oil in a casserole dish and fry the onions and garlic slowly for about 5 minutes. Add the chicken and paprika and continue to fry for a few minutes. Season, add the stock, and simmer for 30 minutes.

Just before serving, stir in the soured cream. Serve with rice or potatoes.

RUSSIAN

Famed for its caviar and vodka, the latter of which tends to be more popular in student circles. The recent opening of a McDonald's store in Moscow has enabled Russians finally to savour a taste of Western culture. And it is such a bargain – for the average Russian a Big Mac will only set them back a year's wages. So it is hardly surprising that the Russians have instead learnt to do 101 things with a potato. In fact, potatoes are their staple diet. So here is a recipe without them.

BEEF STROGANOFF

This recipe traditionally uses fillet steak, but it is unlikely that you will be able to afford it, so rump or even stewing steak could be used as a substitute.

Serves 4

Ingredients

1 lb (500g) of steak
1 large onion, peeled and chopped
1 clove of garlic, peeled and finely chopped
4 oz (100g) of mushrooms, sliced
1 glass of white wine
2 oz (50g) of butter
½ pint (0.25 litre) of soured cream
Salt
Pepper

RUSSIAN

Bash the steak with a rolling pin to flatten it out, but don't get too carried away. Then cut into strips ½ inch (1.5cm) wide and 2 inches (5cm) long. Fry the steak in the butter for about 3 or 4 minutes, then remove from the pan and put in a bowl.

Fry the onions and garlic for 5 minutes, then add the mushrooms and cook until they have softened. Stir in the wine, season, and put the meat back. Cook for about 20 to 30 minutes, stirring occasionally to prevent burning.

Before serving, add the soured cream and heat through.

MEXICAN

The atmospheric temperature is reflected in the food (it's damn hot) and can result in severe aromatic expulsions from the *trasero*.

CHILLI CON CARNE

This tends to go down with students almost as well as a pint of beer. The chilli can be made as hot as required, but remember that even though you may love to sweat, your housemates might prefer it a little milder. It can be served with rice, potatoes or pitta bread.

Serves 4

Ingredients

2 tbs of olive oil
3 tsp of chilli powder
1 or 2 red/green chilli peppers
1 lb (500g) of minced beef
1 large onion, peeled and chopped
2 cloves of garlic, peeled and finely chopped
¼ pint (125ml) of beef stock
1 tin of chopped tomatoes
1 tin of kidney beans, drained
1 tsp of oregano
1 tbs of tomato purée
1 glass of red wine (optional)
Salt
Pepper

MEXICAN

After frying the onions, chilli powder and garlic in the oil for about 5 minutes, add the mince. Cook the mince for about 10 minutes stirring constantly to stop it burning. Add the other ingredients, except the kidney beans, varying the amounts of seasoning according to taste. Bring to the boil then simmer for about 20 minutes (the longer the better). Add the kidney beans 5 minutes before serving.

Serve with rice or jacket potatoes.

NACHOS

Serves 4

Ingredients

2 tbs of olive oil
2 tsp of chilli powder
1 large onion, peeled and chopped
2 cloves of garlic, peeled and finely chopped
1 tin of chopped tomatoes
1 large bag of tortilla chips
4 oz (100g) of cheese, grated
1 tbs of tomato purée
1 green pepper, seeded and finely chopped
Salt
Pepper

Heat the oil in a large saucepan, then fry the onion and garlic for about 3 to 4 minutes. Add the chilli powder and the green pepper and cook for another couple of minutes. Then add the tomatoes, tomato purée and seasoning and cook for about 15 minutes.

Whilst the sauce is cooking, arrange the tortilla chips in a ceramic dish. When the sauce is ready, pour over the chips and finally cover with cheese. Then place under a hot grill until the cheese has melted – enjoy.

SPANISH

If your diet has room to become a little more adventurous than usual, there are plenty of delicious Spanish dishes such as fabada, cocido and, of course, paella which can be washed down with copious quantities of sangria.

PAELLA

This is probably Spain's most well-known dish. It traditionally uses seafood like prawns and mussels, but as these make it expensive for the student they can be left out.

Serves 4 to 5

Ingredients

4 tbs of olive oil
2 onions, peeled and chopped
2 cloves of garlic, peeled and finely chopped
8 oz (200g) of rice
1 green pepper, seeded and cut into pieces
4 oz (100g) of frozen peas
4 tomatoes (seeds removed)
1 pint (0.5 litre) of chicken stock
4 chicken pieces
Pinch of saffron
4 oz (100g) of cooked mussels (optional)
4 oz (100g) of peeled prawns (optional)
Salt
Pepper

Heat half the oil in a large frying pan, or preferably a wok, then fry the onions and garlic for 3 to 4 minutes. Season. Add the rice, saffron, tomatoes and stock, bring to the boil, then cook gently for 10 minutes.

Fry the chicken in a separate pan with the remaining oil for 10 minutes or until lightly browned. Then add the chicken to the rice, stir in the other ingredients, and simmer until the rice is cooked. Serve with lemon wedges.

SPANISH OMELETTE

As there are numerous variations on this meal, don't hold yourself back with what you add.

Serves 4

Ingredients

4 eggs
1 potato, boiled for 10 minutes and chopped
2 tomatoes, sliced
1 oz (25g) of peas
1 onion, peeled and chopped
Mixed herbs
Salt
Pepper

Beat the eggs, season, add the vegetables and pour into a flan dish. Bake at Gas Mark 6 (425 °F, 220 °C) for 15 to 20 minutes or until the mixture ceases to be runny.

Serve with a green salad and a pair of maracas.

AMERICAN

There is actually a lot more to American cuisine than bagels and hotdogs. Americans love to eat, and this is generally reflected in their size, and their obsession with fitness.

BURGERS

This traditional example of American fare has now become one of the world's most popular forms of laxative.

Makes 4 burgers

Ingredients

1 lb (500g) of minced beef
1 onion, peeled and finely chopped
2 oz (50g) of breadcrumbs
1 egg
1 tsp of French mustard
1 clove of garlic, peeled and finely chopped
Dash of tabasco sauce
Dash of Worcester sauce
Salt
Pepper

Throw all the ingredients in a bowl, mix together, and divide the mixture into 4 portions. Shape each portion into something that resembles a burger. Grill for about 4 or 5 minutes on each side on a medium grill, or until golden brown.

JAMBALAYA

The sausages that are used in Cajun cooking are different to the British banger. One of the most widely used is the chorizo variety. These are available in England, but if you can't find any then ordinary sausages will do. It is important to remember that in most recipes the ingredients given are guidelines, and that a lack of one particular item should not preclude you from attempting that recipe (unless, of course, you're trying to make toast without any bread etc). But generally speaking, be brave and make up your own variation or concoction.

Serves 4

Ingredients

2 chicken breasts, cut into pieces
½ lb (250g) of sausage (chorizo if available)
½ lb (250g) of rice
1 onion, peeled and chopped
2 cloves of garlic, peeled and finely chopped
1 green pepper, seeded and chopped
2 sticks of celery, chopped
1 tsp of cayenne pepper
1 pint (0.5 litre) of vegetable/chicken stock
Salt
Pepper

Heat the oil in a large saucepan or a wok. Fry the onion, garlic, sausage and chicken for about 5 minutes, then add the pepper and celery. Continue frying for another couple of minutes, then season and add the cayenne pepper. Pour the stock over the top and bring to the boil.

When the stock is boiling add the rice and cook for roughly 20 minutes or until the rice is soft when pinched. Be careful not to overcook the rice.

MORE FISH

If a recipe uses a whole fish it will need cleaning. This does not mean give it a bubble bath – it means the head, gills and innards have to be removed. Normally fish come already 'cleaned', but, if they don't, ask the fishmonger to do it for you.

Choosing fish is important. Look for the following qualities:

(i) It should not smell.

(ii) The eyes should be bright and full. If the fish is not so fresh the eyes will be dull.

(iii) The gills should be slime-free, clean and shiny.

(iv) If you poke a fresh fish, the flesh will spring back up.

Frozen fish does not tend to have as full a flavour as fresh fish. It is, however, useful to keep a couple of cod fillets in the freezer as they can be cooked fairly quickly and easily.

GRILLED COD

Serves 1

Ingredients

1 cod steak
Butter
Salt
Pepper

Heat the grill. Brush the fish with a little butter, season, and grill for about 10 minutes, according to the size and thickness of the fish, turning once.

If you like a bit more flavour, squeeze some lemon or lime juice on top. Serve with potatoes or rice and fresh vegetables.

BAKED MACKEREL

Serves 2

Ingredients

2 mackerel
2 tsp of mustard
2 tsp of vinegar
2 tbs of water

Clean the mackerel, then score across two or three times on each side. Sprinkle with mustard, vinegar and water. Put the fish in a greased baking tin and bake for 15 to 20 minutes at Gas Mark 5 (400 °F, 200 °C).

BAKED FISH IN WINE

Don't forget the fish!

Serves 2

Ingredients

2 cod steaks
I onion, peeled and cut into rings
I glass of wine, red or white
Salt
Pepper

Put the fish and onions in a shallow baking dish, season, pour the wine over the top and bake in the oven for 35 minutes at Gas Mark 5 (400 °F, 200 °C).

SCOTCH KEDGEREE

Serves 4

Ingredients

8 oz (200g) of rice
1 egg
½ lb (250g) of smoked haddock fillet
2 oz (50g) of butter
2 tbs of fresh parsley, chopped
Juice of 1 lemon
Salt
Pepper

Cook the fish by baking it in the oven for 25 minutes. Then remove from the oven and 'flake' the fish, removing all bones and skin. Cook the rice in boiling water according to the instructions on the packet, which should take roughly 20 to 25 minutes.

Drain and rinse the rice in boiling water – this gets rid of most of the starch. Hard boil the egg by cooking for 10 minutes in boiling water. Then cool, shell and chop into pieces.

Melt the butter in a saucepan and add the fish, then cook for 3 to 4 minutes to reheat it. Stir in the lemon juice, chopped egg, seasoning and rice and serve immediately. Garnish with fresh parsley.

BAKED TROUT

Serves 2

Ingredients

2 small trout, cleaned
I onion, peeled and finely chopped
I carrot, peeled and finely chopped
I clove of garlic, peeled and finely chopped
I oz (25g) of flaked almonds
½ oz (15g) of butter
Salt
Pepper

Melt the butter in a frying pan, then add the onion, carrot and garlic. Fry for about 5 minutes. Place each trout on a piece of tinfoil, making sure the foil is big enough to completely wrap the fish. Divide the vegetables between the two fish, placing the vegetables on the top and the sides of the fish, sprinkle with the almonds, season, then seal up the 'parcels'.

Bake in the oven for about 20 minutes at Gas Mark 5 (400 °F, 200 °C).

Serve with potatoes, rice or salad.

HADDOCK AND ONION BAKE

Serves 4

Ingredients

4 pieces of haddock
1 large onion, peeled and sliced into rings
3 tomatoes, sliced
1 tbs capers, rinsed (optional)
2 oz (50g) of butter
Salt
Pepper

This is an easy dish that should take no more than 5 minutes to prepare. Put the fish and onion in an ovenproof dish with the butter. Season and bake for 15 minutes at Gas Mark 5 (400 °F, 200 °C). Then add the sliced tomatoes and capers and cook for a further 10 minutes.

Serve with potatoes and fresh vegetables.

SKATE WITH SAGE BUTTER

Serves 2

Ingredients

**1 large skate wing
2 tbs of olive oil
1 oz (25g) of butter
2 tsp of capers
Juice of ½ lemon
6 sage leaves
Salt
Pepper**

Heat the oil in a large frying pan, then add the butter and melt. Add the sage leaves and fry gently for 3 minutes, before adding the skate wing. Throw in the capers and lemon juice. Make sure before starting this recipe that your frying pan is big enough to hold the wing.

Cook the skate for about 5 minutes on each side, depending on the thickness. Season. Serve immediately with all the juices from the pan. Delicious with new potatoes.

SPECIAL DIETS

There are going to be occasions when you might need to cater for a friend who is on a 'special diet'. This diet could be as a result of health implications, or it could just mean they are fussy. There would be too many variations to cover all eventualities and there are plenty of specific recipe books available that cater for even the most bizarre of diets.

The Gluten-Free Diet

A gluten-free diet is essential for people who have coeliac disease or dermatitis herpetiformis (a gluten-induced skin sensitivity). Coeliacs suffer from a reaction to gluten, a protein that is found in wheat, rye, barley and, usually, oats.

A gluten-free diet involves the complete avoidance of all foods made from the above. This means that cakes, biscuits, pasta, noodles for instance are all forbidden.

For more information on coeliacs disease take a look at the Coeliac Society website: http://www.coeliac.co.uk

Dairy-Free Diet

Someone who suffers a reaction to lactose is referred to lactose intolerant. It means that they are unable to break down the sugar called lactose that is found in milk. Lactose intolerance can vary in its severity. Some sufferers are intolerant to all dairy products including eggs, others only have a reaction to certain dairy products. If you are having to cater for someone with a lactose intolerance, it would be advisable to steer clear of all dairy products, such as milk, cream, crème fraîche, soured cream and yoghurt. Many manufactured products will have to be avoided too. Cakes, biscuits and ready-meals are all likely to contain dairy products.

For more information see: http://www.lactose.co.uk

Low-Carb Diet

The low-carb diet has made a spectacular comeback into fashion. In simple terms the diet works by cutting down on carbohydrate intake. This means no bread, pasta, rice or potatoes for instance. Some diets also cut out certain high-carb vegetables such as carrots and parsnips. Certain fruits are not recommended either. The good news is that you can stuff yourself with meat, cheese and cream. One of the problems associated with this diet is that it can get very boring. See specialist low-carb cookbooks for inspiration.

VEGETARIAN

Vegetarian food is no longer dismissed as being tasteless lentil-orientated mush with a limp lettuce leaf side dish. The variety of recipes is vast and it is now not uncommon for most people to eat meat-free dishes regularly, without a second thought. Those people who say veggie cooking is boring are the sort of people that eat pie and chips every night and think that a courgette is some sort of American car.

VEGAN OR VEGETARIAN?

A **vegetarian** is someone who excludes meat or meat and fish from their diet, but will often eat dairy products and even eggs. They object to animals being killed for food, and so will not eat parts of dead animals.

A **vegan** eats no animal products at all – not even those produced by living creatures. This rules out dairy butter and cheese etc.

JACKET POTATO

*This is a traditional component of a student diet, probably
due to its low cost and simplicity. It is important to use old
potatoes – new ones are not suitable. This also applies to
roast potatoes.*

Ingredients

1 large potato

After viciously stabbing your potato with a sharp implement
(preferably a fork), bung in the oven for about 60 minutes
at Gas Mark 7 (450 °F, 230 °C).

Test the potato with a skewer or a knife to see if it is
cooked in the middle. For a crispier skin, drizzle a little oil
and salt over the potato before putting it in the oven.

To make the potato more exciting, different fillings can be
added on top, like . . .

- Chilli and cheese
- Coleslaw
- Tuna and mayonnaise
- Baked beans with Worcester sauce and a fried egg
- Cottage cheese and chives

STUFFED CABBAGE

This recipe serves 2. Rabbits, that is.

Ingredients

6 large cabbage leaves
8 oz (200g) of spinach
6 oz (150g) of cooked rice
1 onion, peeled and chopped
2 oz (50g) of butter
4 oz (100g) of cheddar cheese, grated
1 egg yolk
½ pint (0.25 litre) of vegetable stock
Salt
Pepper

First, cook the spinach in a little water for 5 minutes, then drain thoroughly and put aside. Cook the cabbage leaves for about 2 minutes. Melt the butter and add the chopped onion together with the rice, spinach, cheese and seasoning. Bind with the egg yolk.

When thoroughly mixed, put a heaped spoonful of the mixture onto each of the leaves, and wrap it up into a parcel. Place the parcel in an ovenproof dish and pour the stock on top. Cover with foil and bake for 30 minutes at Gas Mark 4 (350 °F, 180 °C).

LENTIL CURRY

Serves 2

Ingredients

2 tbs of olive oil
4 oz (100g) of lentils soaked in cold water for 1 hour
½ pint (0.25 litre) of vegetable stock
4 carrots, peeled and chopped
1 onion, peeled and chopped
1 courgette, sliced
1 leek, sliced
1 tbs of curry powder
2 fresh tomatoes, sliced
Salt
Pepper

Boil the lentils for about 7 minutes and then drain. Heat the oil in a large saucepan, then fry the onions and curry powder for 5 minutes. Add the other vegetables, season and fry for another 5 minutes. Add the stock and lentils, bring to the boil, then simmer for 1 hour. Serve with rice.

LEEKS WITH CHEESE

Serves 4

Ingredients

**2 lb (1kg) of leeks
4 oz (100g) of cheddar cheese
Salt
Pepper**

Chop off the ends of the leeks and slice the whitish bit into rings about ½ inch (1.5cm) thick. Wash to remove any grit. Boil in water for about 5 minutes then drain. Place in an ovenproof dish, season, cover with cheese, and grill until the cheese has melted.

RATATOUILLE

This traditional Provençal recipe can really be made from whatever vegetables are available. Tinned tomatoes are cheaper than buying fresh ones (except in the summer when fresh ones are more affordable).
The lemon is considered optional by some, but I believe it to be essential.

Serves 4

Ingredients

2 tbs of olive oil
I tin of chopped tomatoes
2 onions, peeled and finely chopped
2 cloves of garlic, peeled and finely chopped
I small aubergine, chopped
I red pepper, seeded and chopped
I courgette, thinly sliced
I lemon, quartered (optional)
2 tsp of rosemary
I bay leaf
I glass of red wine, water or tomato juice (optional)
Salt
Pepper

Before you prepare the other vegetables, place the pieces of aubergine on a plate and sprinkle them with salt. After preparing the vegetables, wash the aubergine pieces then dry them with kitchen paper. Heat the oil in a large saucepan. Fry the onions and garlic for about 5 minutes, then add the courgette, the aubergine and the pepper. Cook for about 5 minutes then add the tomatoes, lemon and other ingredients. Bring to the boil and then simmer for 20 minutes.

Ratatouille can be served with almost anything – rice, baked potato, pitta bread etc. It can also be served cold.

VEGETABLE KEBABS

Serves 2

Ingredients

1 pepper, seeded and cut into pieces
1 courgette, cut into chunks
1 small onion, peeled and quartered
2 tomatoes, quartered
4 mushrooms, halved or quartered
1 oz (25g) of butter
Salt
Pepper

Thread all the vegetables onto a couple of skewers and daub them with butter, then grill for about 15 minutes. For a different flavour try adding a tablespoon of runny honey or a dash of soy sauce whilst grilling. Season and serve with rice.

PASTA WITH PINE KERNELS AND SULTANAS

This recipe is very easy to prepare and tastes wonderful, unless the wrong sort of oil is used.

Serves 4

Ingredients

**8 tbs of olive oil
10 oz (250g) of pasta
2 cloves of garlic, peeled and finely chopped
2 oz (50g) of sultanas
2 oz (50g) of pine kernels
Salt
Pepper**

Cook the pasta of your choice according to the instructions on the packet. Drain the pasta and place in a serving bowl. Pour the oil over the pasta then stir in the garlic, pine kernels and sultanas. Season, then serve immediately. Parmesan can be added on top if required.

CLARE'S NUTTY RICE

This recipe is best cooked in a large wok, but a saucepan or a dustbin lid will do.

Serves 2 to 4

Ingredients

2 tbs of olive oil
2 cups of wholemeal rice
1 green pepper, seeded and chopped
1 small tin of sweetcorn
1 onion, peeled and chopped
1 oz (25g) of mushrooms, sliced
1 clove of garlic, peeled and finely chopped
4 oz (100g) of walnuts
1 vegetarian stock cube
Fresh parsley
Salt
Pepper

Heat the oil in a large frying pan or wok then fry the onion and garlic for between 4 and 5 minutes. Add the mushrooms, green pepper and sweetcorn and fry for another couple of minutes. Next add the uncooked rice and about 4 cups of water. Sprinkle the stock cube over the mixture and stir frequently. Simmer for about 20 minutes, depending on the type of rice used. Add more water if necessary to stop the rice from drying out.

If the rice is soft when pinched then it is cooked. Add the walnuts a couple of minutes before removing from the heat. Season with salt and pepper.

PARSLEY AND PASTA

Serves 2

Ingredients

4 oz (100g) of wholemeal pasta shells
1 oz (25g) of butter
1 or 2 oz (25 or 50g) of cheddar cheese, grated
3 tbs fresh parsley, roughly chopped
Salt
Pepper

Cook the pasta according to the instructions on the packet, then drain. Add the butter and allow it to melt. Add the salt, pepper, cheese and parsley, and toss until evenly distributed, then serve immediately.

VEGETARIAN LASAGNE

You can use a meat substitute with this recipe, called silken tofu. It sounds like a Greek island, but it tastes a bit better than that. If you can find some, prepare in the same way as the meat lasagne (see Italian), substituting the meat for tofu. Reduce the cooking time, though.

Serves 4

Ingredients

2 tbs of olive oil
1 large onion, peeled and chopped
1 red pepper, seeded and chopped
1 green pepper, seeded and chopped
1 clove of garlic, peeled and finely chopped
1 leek, finely chopped
2 courgettes, finely sliced
1 tin of chopped tomatoes
2 tbs of tomato purée
2 tsp of oregano
Salt
Pepper
1 packet of lasagne (no pre-cooking required type)

For the cheese sauce:

1 oz (25g) of butter
2 oz (50g) of flour
1 pint (0.5 litre) of milk
6 oz (150g) of cheese, grated

Heat the oil in a large saucepan and add the onion and garlic. Cook for 5 minutes, then stir in the leek, peppers and courgette, frying gently for another 3 minutes or so. Then add the tomatoes, purée, oregano and seasoning, bring to the boil then simmer for a further 20 minutes. While the vegetable sauce is simmering prepare the cheese sauce.

Melt the butter in a saucepan and add the flour, stirring constantly. Remove from the heat and add the milk in stages. Then bring to the boil and add the cheese, saving a bit for the top. Simmer for 3 or 4 minutes. Add more flour if the sauce refuses to thicken.

Grease a shallow baking dish, then add a layer of vegetable sauce, a layer of lasagne, a layer of cheese sauce, a layer of lasagne, and so on, making sure to end up with cheese sauce on top. Then sprinkle on the remaining cheese.

Bake in a preheated oven for around 25 minutes at Gas Mark 6 (425 °F, 220 °C).

SALADS

There are endless recipes for salads, and most people have worked out their own special combinations.

There is an increasing amount of more exotic salad stuff around; some supermarkets stock up to ten different varieties of lettuce alone. But salads are still more popular during the summer months when the produce is cheaper.

Here are some of my favourite recipes.

PASTA SALAD

Salad with an Italian feel.

Serves 3 to 4

Ingredients

4 oz (100g) of pasta quills or shells
1 red pepper, seeded and chopped
7 oz (175g) tin of tuna
3 tomatoes, sliced
French dressing (optional)
Salt
Pepper

Boil some water in a saucepan and cook the pasta for about 15 minutes or until it is tender, then drain.

Drain the oil from the tuna then mix the ingredients in a serving bowl. Add 2 to 3 tablespoons of dressing if required.

See Dressing and Sauces for a recipe for French dressing.

RICE AND SWEETCORN

Ingredients

8 oz (200g or 1 mug) of rice
9 oz (225g) tin of sweetcorn
1 green pepper, seeded and chopped into pieces
4 tomatoes, finely chopped
French dressing (see Dressings and Sauces)
Salt
Pepper

Wash the rice in a sieve to remove some of the starch. Put the rice in a large saucepan with about a pint of water and a pinch of salt. After the water has boiled, simmer for about 20 to 25 minutes or until the rice is tender, then drain well. Mix all the other ingredients with the rice and pour a little French dressing on top.

SALADE NIÇOISE

Serves 4

Ingredients

1 lettuce
3 tomatoes
2 eggs
8 oz (200g) tin of tuna
6 oz (150g) cooked French beans
6 anchovy fillets
10 black olives
French dressing (see Dressings and Sauces)
Salt
Pepper

Hard boil the eggs for 8 minutes, then place in a bowl of cold water. Wash the lettuce and arrange the leaves in a large serving bowl, then add the tuna (drain the oil first) and toss it all together.

Quarter the tomatoes and place them on top of the lettuce. Shell the eggs, cut them into quarters, and arrange them neatly on top. Pour the dressing over the salad, and add the olives, beans and anchovies, if required. Season.

TOMATO AND ONION

A typical Provençal salad.

Serves 4

Ingredients

4 fresh tomatoes
1 onion
Fresh basil
French dressing (see Dressings and Sauces)
Salt
Pepper

Peel the onion and slice fairly thinly. Slice the tomatoes and arrange them on a large plate or dish. Place the onion pieces between the tomato slices. Decorate with the basil leaves, and season well. Pour the French dressing over the top.

POTATO SALAD

Chopped fresh chives or coriander can be added if required.

Serves 2

Ingredients

6 medium-sized new potatoes
1 oz (25g) of butter
Mayonnaise
Salt
Pepper

If you are using new potatoes the skins can be left on them, otherwise they must be peeled. Place the potatoes in boiling water for 15 minutes or until a knife will pass through the centre fairly easily. After the potatoes have cooled, cut into 1-inch (2.5cm) cubes and place in a bowl with butter. When the potatoes have cooled add a good coating of mayonnaise. Mix together and season.

Chopped fresh chives or coriander can be added if you like. If you are using small new potatoes they can be left whole. Another alternative to using mayonnaise is to place new potatoes in a bowl with a couple of tablespoons of olive oil.

AVOCADO AND FRENCH DRESSING

Avocado is a calorie watcher's nightmare, so if you are trying to slim don't be tempted by this recipe. When choosing an avocado to be eaten straight away make sure it is ripe – it should be slightly soft when the skin is pressed.

Ingredients

1 avocado
French dressing (see Dressings and Sauces)

Remove the skin of the avocado using a knife. Then cut in half, remembering that it is not possible to cut all the way through because there is an avocado stone in the middle. Cut around the stone, then pull the two halves away from each other. The stone will stay lodged in one side. The easiest way of removing the stone is to stick a sharp knife in it and then ease it out.

After removing the stone, cut the avocado into slices then cover with dressing. Eat immediately.

TABBOULEH

Bulghur wheat is made from wheat that has been boiled, dried, then ground. As an ingredient it is widely used in countries like Morocco and Tunisia.

Serves 4

Ingredients

6 oz (150g) of bulghur wheat
4 tbs of olive oil
½ cucumber, chopped
1 tomato, peeled and chopped
1 bunch of spring onions
1 bunch of parsley
8 mint leaves, chopped
Juice of 1 lemon
Salt
Pepper

Place the bulghur wheat in a saucepan of water. Bring to the boil, then simmer gently for 10 to 15 minutes until tender. Drain, then allow to cool.

Finely chop the parsley and the spring onions. Place the bulghur in a serving bowl, add the olive oil, parsley, mint, tomato, cucumber, spring onions, lemon juice, salt and pepper. Mix together thoroughly.

SMOKED SALMON SALAD

Serves 4

Ingredients

Mixed salad
4 oz (100g) smoked salmon
1 lemon, cut into wedges
Salt
Pepper
Olive oil

Arrange the mixed salad on four small plates so that the plates are covered. Cut the salmon into small pieces then place on the salad leaves. Drizzle lightly with olive oil, then season. Serve with the lemon wedges.

SNACKS AND MIDNIGHT CRAVINGS

This is another essential section, since often when breakfast or lunch is skipped a snack can keep the hunger at bay until the evening meal. It is interesting to compare what people regard as a 'snack': for some it is a plate of chips, a pile of sandwiches and a couple of doughnuts, while for others it could be half an apple.

B.L.T.

Otherwise known as a bacon, lettuce and tomato sandwich. Note that this is not your everyday type of sarnie – this is heading towards the realms of haute cuisine, mate!

Serves 1

Ingredients

Butter
3 slices of bread
2 rashers of bacon
1 to 2 lettuce leaves
1 tomato
Salt
Pepper

Remove the crusts from the bread, then slice the tomato. Grill the bacon and the bread. Butter the toast, then place a bit of lettuce, some tomato and a rasher of bacon on it. Put a slice of toast on top and then make up another layer as before. Finish with the last piece of toast on top, then cut diagonally across. Add a dash of salt, pepper and a little mayonnaise if required.

To stop the B.L.T. from falling apart you could try skewering it with a cocktail stick. But under no circumstances should you swallow the cocktail stick in your haste to eat your masterpiece – they are not particularly palatable.

BACON AND CHEESE

This for me is the ultimate sandwich . . . simple, but devastating.

Serves 1

Ingredients

**2 slices of bread
2 rashers of bacon
Cheddar cheese
Butter
Tomato sauce**

Grill the bacon for a couple of minutes on each side, longer if you prefer it crispy. Whilst the bacon is being grilled, butter the bread and cut a few slices of cheese. When the bacon is cooked place on the bread with the cheese, then squirt some tomato sauce inside – lovely.

CHEESE ON TOAST

A very popular lunchtime snack that can be prepared with tomato on top.

Serves 1

Ingredients

Bread
Cheese

Toast one side of the bread and cover the other side with a thick layer of cheddar cheese. Then grill gently until the cheese browns or begins to bubble. Remove from grill, cut in half, and eat immediately before rapid cooling sets in. Great with a splash of Worcester or tabasco sauce.

WELSH RAREBIT

Doesn't taste particularly Welsh, nor is it very rare.

Serves 1

Ingredients

6 oz (150g) of cheddar cheese
½ oz (15g) of butter
½ tsp of dry mustard
2 tbs of flour
2 slices of bread
4 rashers of streaky bacon

Grate the cheese and put into a small saucepan. Add the butter and mustard, then cook gently, stirring constantly, until the cheese has melted. Take the saucepan away from the heat and add the flour, beating it in until smooth. Allow to cool.

Grill the bacon and the bread, then spread the cheese mixture evenly over the toast. Grill until golden, then add the bacon and serve.

PLAIN OMELETTE

Serves 1 to 2

Ingredients

2 or 3 eggs
Pinch of mixed herbs
Salt
Pepper
1 oz (25g) of butter

Beat the eggs together in a mixing bowl and add the seasoning. Melt the butter in a frying pan and pour in the eggs.

As soon as the eggs start to cook, lift up one edge of the omelette with a spatula, tilt the pan and let the uncooked egg run underneath. Continue to do this until the omelette is cooked, then flip it in half and serve on a warmed plate.

CHEESE AND TOMATO OMELETTE

Serves 1 to 2

Ingredients

2 or 3 eggs
2 oz (50g) of cheese, grated
1 oz (25g) of butter
1 tomato, chopped
Salt
Pepper

Prepare as for the previous recipe, but add the cheese and tomato before pouring into the frying pan.

BACON OMELETTE

Serves 1 to 2

Ingredients

2 or 3 eggs
2 rashers of bacon
1 oz (25g) of butter
Salt
Pepper

Cut the bacon up into little pieces and fry for a couple of minutes, then remove from the pan. Beat the eggs together, season and add the bacon. Melt the butter in the frying pan and cook using the method described for the plain omelette.

EGG AND CHEESE RAMEKINS

Serves 1

Ingredients

2 oz (50g) of cheese, grated
1 egg
1 tomato
1 tsp of butter
Salt
Pepper

Using the butter grease a small ovenproof dish, preferably a ramekin dish or one that is about 3 inches (7.5cm) in diameter. Put grated cheese in the bottom of the dish and up the sides. Place a slice of tomato inside and then the egg, trying not to break the yolk. Add the seasoning and cover with another slice of tomato and more grated cheese.

Bake in the oven for about 15 minutes at Gas Mark 4 (350 °F, 180 °C) or until the egg is set.

POTATO AND ONION FRY

Serves 4

Ingredients

1 lb (500g) of potatoes
1 onion
4 rashers of bacon
2 tbs of vegetable oil
1 tbs of plain flour
2 eggs, beaten
Salt
Pepper

Peel the onion and potatoes, then coarsely grate them and place in a mixing bowl. Add the beaten eggs, bacon and flour, mix together, then season. Heat the oil in a frying pan, then spoon a series of heaped tablespoons of the mixture into the pan. Fry the potato cakes on both sides till they turn a golden brown. Continue doing this until all the mixture is used up.

Serve with baked beans or a salad.

PUDS, BICCIES AND CAKES

VICTORIA SPONGE

Two 7-inch sandwich tins are needed for this recipe.

Ingredients

**6 oz (150g) of self-raising flour
6 oz (150g) of butter
6 oz (150g) of caster sugar
3 eggs
Jam**

Mix together the sugar and butter until they are smooth in texture. Gradually add the eggs to the mixture, then fold in the flour. Divide the mixture between the 2 baking tins (these need to be greased first, which means wiping the inside with a piece of greaseproof paper covered with butter). Make sure that the tops of the cakes are level, then bake in the oven for 20 minutes or so at Gas Mark 5 (400 °F, 200 °C).

The way to see if a cake is cooked is to stick a skewer or a knitting needle (if you don't happen to have either to hand then a knife will do) into the centre of the sponge. If bits of the mixture are stuck to it when it is drawn out, the cake needs to be cooked a little longer. If the skewer comes out clean, the cake is ready.

Now turn the cakes out of the tins onto a wire rack (look in the grill pan for one). Once cooled, spread your favourite jam over one of the layers, sandwich the other one on top, and sprinkle with caster sugar.

ROCK BUNS

Ingredients

8 oz (200g) of self-raising flour
4 oz (100g) of butter
3 oz (75g) of currants or raisins
Pinch of nutmeg
3 oz (75g) of sugar
1 egg, beaten
2 tbs of milk
Pinch of salt

Mix the flour, nutmeg and salt together. Then rub the flour and butter together until they look like breadcrumbs. The next stage is to add the currants, sugar, egg and milk. The mixture should be fairly firm.

Grease a baking tray with some butter. Mould the mixture into small lumps and place on the baking tray.
Bake for 20 minutes at Gas Mark 6 (425 °F, 220 °C).

ICED CHOCOLATE CAKE

Two 7-inch sandwich tins are needed for this recipe.

Ingredients

6 oz (150g) of self-raising flour
6 oz (150g) of butter
6 oz (150g) of caster sugar
3 eggs
1 ½ oz (40g) of cocoa
1 ½ tbs of water

For the icing:

8 oz (200g) of icing sugar
4 oz (100g) of plain cooking chocolate
1 ½ oz (40g) of butter
2 tbs of warm water

Place the sugar and the butter in a large mixing bowl and mix together, using either a wooden spoon or an electric mixer (which will save time). Add the eggs, one at a time.

In a separate bowl, mix the flour and the cocoa powder together, then add it to the creamed mixture. Continue mixing, adding water until a soft dropping consistency is achieved. Divide the mixture equally between two 7-inch sandwich tins, which have been greased first. Bake in the oven at Gas Mark 5 (400 °F, 200 °C) for 25 to 30 minutes.

Test the cake with a skewer. If the mixture sticks to it, the cake needs a few more minutes in the oven.

When the cakes are ready, turn them out of their tins onto a wire rack (if available). Melt the chocolate by placing it in a basin and putting that over the top of a saucepan of boiling water. Be careful not to let the water boil over the top of the saucepan into the chocolate.

After the chocolate has melted, allow to cool. Cream together the butter and half the icing sugar, then add half the melted chocolate. Mix, and spread over one side of the cake, then 'sandwich' the two together.

The rest of the chocolate is used to make the icing on the top. Add the water and remaining sugar to the chocolate, and spoon onto the top of the cake. Spread the icing around using a palette knife that has been dipped in hot water (this helps to spread the icing and stop it sticking to the knife). The cake can be decorated with those little silver balls that break your teeth, or with tasteful designs of snooker tables etc.

BAKED APPLES

Ingredients

I large cooking apple per person
Mincemeat
Brown sugar
Butter

Remove the cores from the apples and stand them in an ovenproof dish. Fill the hole in the apple with mincemeat and a teaspoon of brown sugar. Add a nob of butter on top. Put enough water in the dish to cover the bottom of the apples. Bake at Gas Mark 4 (350 °F, 180 °C) for about an hour. Then test the apple with a skewer. It should be soft, but not too soft. Serve with cream.

GRANDMA'S CHOCOLATE CHIP COOKIES

This is one of my Grandmother's recipes. I would like to thank her for the regular supply of these cookies and all the other things she makes for me.

Ingredients

6 oz (150g) of self-raising flour
3 oz (75g) of butter
3 oz (75g) of granulated sugar
1 oz (25g) of brown sugar
2 drops of vanilla essence
4 oz (100g) of cooking chocolate
1 egg

Cream the butter and the sugars either in a mixer or with a wooden spoon. Beat in the egg and vanilla. Grate or chop the chocolate coarsely, then stir into the creamed mixture with the flour. Using a teaspoon make into balls and place on a greased flat baking tin. Bake in the centre of the oven for about 15 minutes at Gas Mark 5 (400 °F, 200 °C). Place on a wire tray and leave until cold.

RASPBERRY BUNS

Ingredients

Raspberry jam
8 oz (200g) of self-raising flour
4 oz (100g) of caster sugar
3 oz (75g) of butter
1 egg, beaten
1 tbs of milk
Pinch of salt

Rub the butter and flour together, using your fingertips, until the mixture resembles breadcrumbs. Add the sugar, egg, salt and milk, and mix well. The mixture should be quite stiff.

Grease a baking tray, then shape the mixture into twelve balls and place on the tray. Make a little hole on the top and fill with a teaspoon of jam.

Bake in the oven at Gas Mark 6 (425 °F, 220 °C) for about 20 minutes.

FLAPJACKS

For those with access to two baking trays and living in a large household it can be advisable to double the quantities given here, as flapjacks tend to be incredibly popular.

Ingredients

8 oz (200g) of porridge oats
4 oz (100g) of butter
3 oz (75g) of sugar
4 level tbs of golden syrup
Pinch of salt

Melt the butter in a large saucepan, then add the syrup and leave over a low heat for a couple of minutes. Remove from the heat and add the sugar, salt and oats. Mix thoroughly using a wooden spoon, making sure all the oats are covered with syrup.

Grease a shallow baking tray and evenly spoon in the mixture. Cook for 20 to 30 minutes at Gas Mark 4 (350 °F, 180 °C). After cooking, cut the flapjacks into bars before they cool.

SCONES

Ingredients

**8 oz (200g) of self-raising flour
2 oz (50g) of butter
¼ pint (125ml) of milk
Pinch of salt**

Mix the flour and salt together. The flour is supposed to be sieved, but it's a bit time-consuming and doesn't make much difference anyway. Cut the butter into small cubes and add them to the flour. Rub the mixture using your fingers, continuing until the result looks like breadcrumbs.

Add the milk and stir in using the blade of a knife to form a soft dough. Roll out the mixture on a floured board until it is about ½ inch (1.5cm) thick. Cut into rounds using a biscuit cutter or a glass.

Grease a baking tray and place some scones on it, leaving big enough gaps for them to rise. Brush some milk over the top of the scones to obtain a smooth and shiny finish.

Bake in the oven for 10 to 15 minutes at Gas Mark 7 (450 °F, 230 °C).

Cheese Scones

As for plain scones, but stir in 4 oz (100g) of cheese before adding the milk.

Fruit Scones

As for plain scones, but stir in 1 oz (25g) of sugar and 2 oz (50g) of dried fruit, sultanas, currants etc.

BAKED BANANAS

Ingredients

1 banana
Brown or golden granulated sugar
Lemon juice

Preheat the oven to Gas Mark 4 (350 °F, 180 °C). Peel the banana and place it on a piece of foil, shiny side uppermost, making sure the foil is large enough to wrap it up loosely. Squeeze the lemon juice over the banana, sprinkle with brown sugar, and loosely wrap up.

Place in the centre of the oven on a baking tray and bake until it is slightly soft to touch.

Serve with cream or ice cream.

LEMON SNOW

Serves 4 to 6

Ingredients

2 lemons
3 tbs of sugar
2 tsp of gelatine
2 egg whites

Grate the lemon rind and squeeze the juice from the lemons. Place the juice and the rind in a small bowl, add the sugar, and sprinkle gelatine on top. Leave until it becomes spongy.

Place the bowl in a saucepan of hot water and heat until the gelatine has dissolved, stirring occasionally. Make sure the water doesn't boil over into the juice. Leave to cool.

Beat the egg whites until stiff, then fold in the gelatine mixture and pile into small dishes or one large bowl.

Decorate with grated chocolate.

RASPBERRY BRÛLÉ

Serves 4

Ingredients

½ lb (250g) of fresh raspberries
½ pint (0.25 litre) of double cream
6 oz (150g) of demerara or golden granulated sugar

Place the raspberries in a shallow heatproof dish. Whip the cream until thick, (but not too stiff) and spread over the raspberries. Sprinkle the sugar over the cream, covering it completely.

Preheat the grill and then place the dish under the grill, until it is dark and bubbling.

Remove from the grill and cool. Chill in the fridge for a couple of hours.

A cheaper version could be made using sliced banana.

POACHED PEACHES

Serves 4

Ingredients

1 tin of peach halves
½ oz (15g) of butter
2 tbs of brown or golden granulated sugar
1 tbs of brandy or whisky (optional)

Drain the syrup from the peaches, reserving a small amount. Melt the butter in a saucepan. Add the peaches with the syrup and sugar.

Heat gently for about 5 minutes then stir in any flavouring. If you have any flaked almonds or nuts, a few of these toasted and sprinkled on top will add great excitement to your life.

BATTERS

YORKSHIRE PUDDING

Ingredients

4 oz (100g) of plain flour
1 egg, beaten
½ pint (0.25 litre) of milk, or milk and water
Oil
Pinch of salt

Mix the salt and flour in a mixing bowl, then make a 'well' in the flour and add the egg. Mix together carefully, adding the milk little by little. Beat the mixture for a few minutes until it is smooth. Pour a teaspoon of oil into individual patty tins, then add 2 tablespoons of the mixture into each. Bake for about 15 minutes or until they have risen and browned.

PANCAKES

Serves 4

Ingredients

4 oz (100g) of plain flour
1 egg
½ pint (0.25 litre) of milk
Pinch of salt
Butter
Sugar (or any other topping)

Put the flour and salt in a bowl and add the egg into the middle. Pour in about a third of the milk. Stir gently, adding a little more milk in the process. Beat the mixture thoroughly, then add the rest of the milk. Stir well, then pour into a jug.

Melt a small piece of butter in a frying pan, then add a couple of tablespoons of the batter. Tip the frying pan to spread the mixture evenly. Fry until the underside is brown, then toss the pancake.

Scrape the mess from the dropped pancake off the floor, then start again. This time, when the underside is brown, turn it over with a fish slice or a knife and cook the other side.

Tip the finished pancake onto a plate and cover with lemon juice and sugar.

PINEAPPLE IN BATTER

This is a nice and easy pud, and can also be made using a banana – just slice the banana lengthways and dip it in the batter, then fry until golden.

Serves 4

Ingredients

**4 oz (100g) of plain flour
1 egg
¼ pint (125ml) of milk
1 tin of pineapple rings
2 tbs of oil**

Prepare the mixture as with the pancakes, then dip a pineapple ring in the batter and fry until the batter turns a golden brown.

BREAKFAST TIME

Supposedly the most important meal of the day, but all too often rushed or ignored altogether. Eggs are a good choice for this meal (in moderation) as they are full of protein.

SCRAMBLED EGGS

Serves 2

Ingredients

3 eggs
I oz (25g) of butter
4 tbs of milk
Pepper

Whisk the eggs in a bowl and add the milk and pepper. Melt the butter in a saucepan and add the egg mixture. Stir the mixture as it thickens. Don't have the heat up too high, or else the egg will burn and stick to the pan.

Serve on top of hot buttered toast.

POACHED EGGS

Ingredients

1 egg per person
Butter

If you have a 'poaching ring' then put in a nob of butter and the egg and cook for about 4 minutes, according to taste. Alternatively, use the more traditional way of poaching eggs: boil some water in a saucepan and then, having broken an egg into a cup or mug, slide the egg into the water. Only put one egg in at a time.

BOILED EGG

Ingredients

1 egg

Boil some water in a saucepan and carefully lower the egg into the water, using a spoon. Then boil for 3 to 4 minutes, depending on how runny you want the egg to be.

After removing the egg from the water, whack the top with a spoon – this will stop the egg from hardening.

If you require the egg to be hard-boiled, cook for about 8 minutes in boiling water.

If your egg cracks whilst it is cooking, pour a tablespoon of vinegar in the water – this will seal the crack.

FRIED EGG

Ingredients

1 egg
2 tbs of oil

Pour some oil in a frying pan, but don't let the fat get too hot or the egg will stick to the pan and bubble. Crack the egg on the side of the pan and plop the egg into the oil. Fry gently for about 3 minutes, basting occasionally. If you like your eggs American-style (sunny side down), fry both sides of the egg.

EGGY BREAD

Ingredients

3 eggs
4 tbs of milk
Slices of bread without the crusts
2 tbs of oil
Pepper

Beat the eggs and the milk together and season. Heat the oil in a frying pan. Dip a slice of bread in the egg mixture and then fry for a couple of minutes on each side.

CONCLUSION

Well, it's the end of the book. Presumably you've bothered to read the rest of it before wondering what this page is all about? No? Well, go and read it, because I want to talk only to those who have been on a culinary journey with me, a journey that has taken us through many fine countries of the world, and a journey on which only the finest food was eaten . . .

You are now a well-travelled (gastronomically speaking) student cook, and are probably full from trying so many wonderful recipes. The only thing to do now is to remember that these recipes should remain part of your diet after you leave college and are forced to discover the real world. Life will get tough, pressures will increase, the daily dose of stress will become as common as the daily sessions of *Neighbours*, but deep down you will know that when you get home you will be able to cook a fine meal. Alternatively, why not escape from the real world altogether and make up a barrel of punch?

Whatever happens, I hope this book has been as entertaining as it has been useful, and that after reading it your housemates will be astounded by your newly acquired culinary skill and imagination. Let's just hope you don't make them sick, anyway.

Bon appétit!

INDEX

STUDENT GRUB

www.summersdale.com